SUMMER SPARKLERS

60 SUNSHINE COCKTAILS FOR SPRING AND SUMMER

JASSY DAVIS

ILLUSTRATED BY SARAH FERONE

HarperCollins*Publishers*

Dedicated to James, Laura and Victoria,
who have always encouraged me

HarperCollins*Publishers*
1 London Bridge Street
London SE1 9GF

www.harpercollins.co.uk

First published by HarperCollins*Publishers* in 2023

HarperCollins*Publishers*
Macken House, 39/40 Mayor Street Upper
Dublin 1, D01 C9W8

3 5 7 9 10 8 6 4 2

Copyright © 2023 HarperCollins*Publishers*
Written by Jassy Davis
Cover and interior illustrations by Sarah Ferone
Cover and interior design by Jacqui Caulton

Jassy Davis asserts the moral right to be
identified as the author of this work

A catalogue record for this book is
available from the British Library

ISBN 978-0-00-860177-5

Printed and bound in Malaysia

DISCLAIMER: The publisher urges readers to drink responsibly.

This book features recipes that include the optional use of raw eggs.
Consuming raw eggs may increase the risk of food-borne illness. Individuals
who are immunocompromised, pregnant or elderly should use caution.
Ensure eggs are fresh and meet local food-standard requirements.

MIX
Paper | Supporting
responsible forestry
FSC™ C007454
FSC
www.fsc.org

This book contains FSC™ certified paper and other controlled
sources to ensure responsible forest management.

For more information visit: www.harpercollins.co.uk/green

Contents

Introduction

On a warm, sunny day, is there a better sound than ice clinking in a glass? I can't think of one, unless it's the pop of a cork or the gentle hiss of a well-chilled soda. In summer an icy drink is an everyday essential, whether it's a boozy mixed drink or a zero-proof refresher. In the afternoon we can linger over pitchers of iced tea in the garden or indulge in coconut-heavy cocktails on the beach. There are zesty sundowners on the balcony, wine coolers at festivals and frosty beers at barbecues that we can all enjoy. Whatever the occasion, there's always a drink that will take the heat out of the day while putting a little pep in your step.

When I started imagining the kind of cocktails I wanted to write about in this book, I began by thinking about all the flavours that I associate with summer. Ripe fruits, lush herbs and sweetly fragranced flowers flourish at this time of year, and I've included lots of them throughout these recipes. While dried spices add warmth and heat to winter drinks, the summer is all about bright tastes and delicate aromas that sparkle in every sip.

I also drew on drinking traditions from around the world. Coming from a damp and rainy part of Northern Europe, my summer is often fleeting and the choice of drinks is sparse. But plenty of other countries bask in golden sunshine and know the value of a tall, crisp and refreshing summer drink. From Caribbean punches, French apéritifs and Spanish sangrias to Indian soft drinks, Italian spritzes and Mexican sodas, the world is bursting with thirst-quenching cocktails that are fun to make.

If you're new to mixing cocktails, summer is a great time of year to start. There are normally plenty of social occasions when you can try out a new drink on your friends, and the kind of cocktails that suit the summer are usually easy to make. Lots of the drinks in this book are built in the glass, so you don't even need to buy much in the way of bar equipment. But if you do want to polish up your techniques and invest in beautiful glassware, there is information here to help you with that, too.

The ingredients should also be easy to find. Your local grocer and supermarket will stock most of them, especially when they're in season (not that tequila goes out of season too often). And there's always the internet if anything does prove a bit tricky. I wanted to make these cocktails as accessible as possible, because if there's one thing a summer drink should always be, it's fun.

The Right Tools for the Job

You can mix drinks at home without buying a single piece of cocktail-making equipment. A jam jar makes a decent shaker, while a pitcher and tablespoon can stand in for a mixing glass, or it can be fun to kit out a home bar with a few stylish bits and pieces. Use this guide to decide what you want to invest in first, and what items you're happy to improvise.

MIXING GLASS

This should be wide enough to let you keep the bar spoon moving and deep enough to contain the cocktail without it spilling over the top. A glass with a heavy base is more stable and won't topple over if you get a bit carried away. Etched mixing glasses provide a bit more grip, so the glass is less likely to slip out of your hand when you pour out the drink. A spout will also help you get the cocktail into the serving glass without spillage.

BAR SPOON

To go with your mixing glass, you'll need a bar spoon. These are long-stemmed spoons that typically have a 2.5–5ml (½–1 teaspoon) bowl. There are three types of bar spoon: American, European and Japanese. American bar spoons are the simplest, with a rubber cap on the end of the spoon and a twisted section in the middle. Great when you're starting out and just want something to stir drinks with. European bar spoons often have round flat discs on the end, which can be used to muddle soft fruits. The stems are twisted all the way down, and you can use them to layer drinks by trickling the spirit down the stem. Japanese bar spoons tend to have teardrop- or pearl-shaped tips and are much longer than their American and European counterparts, making them a lot more theatrical and elegant to use.

JIGGER

A jigger is an hourglass-shaped measurer that has two measuring bowls – the standard jigger (45ml/1½fl oz) and the pony (30ml/1fl oz). These are the basic measurements for cocktail making. You can also buy small measuring glasses that are marked up with millimetres, fluid ounces, tablespoons and teaspoons. I have been known to use a digital scale when I don't want the extra washing up –  just add the glass and ice to the scale, then slowly pour in your spirit – although be warned, this method can lead to some generous over-serves...

SHAKER

There are three types of shaker to choose from:
- The cobbler shaker is a three-part metal shaker that breaks down into a shaking tin, a fitted lid with a strainer built in, and a cap. Because of the integral strainer it's perfect for beginners who don't want to buy a separate strainer.
- The French shaker comes in two pieces and is shaped like the cobbler, but without the integral strainer.
- The Boston shaker is the classic two-piece shaker consisting of a large shaking tin (often metal) and a smaller shaking tin (often glass, and called the pint glass). This shaker is a little trickier to use because you have to make sure you create a seal between the two tins before starting to shake. It also doesn't come with a strainer.

Whichever shaker you go for, pick one you feel comfortable holding and that you can shake and open with confidence.

STRAINERS

If you're using a cobbler shaker you might not think you need to buy a strainer, but a separate strainer can come in really handy – especially when shaking cocktails with fruit or herbs, which can clog up the cobbler's integral strainer.

7

A Hawthorne strainer is the one most of us are familiar with. It's a metal disc with a coiled spring attached to it that will catch large chunks of fruit or ice while the cocktail is being poured out. The Hawthorne strainer is perfect for straining cocktails from a shaker tin.

For straining cocktails from a mixing glass, try a Julep strainer. The strainer has a handle and its bowl has holes stamped in it. Originally, Julep drinkers would hold this kind of strainer over their Julep cocktail when they took a sip, so they didn't end up with a face full of ice and mint. After the invention of the straw, the Julep strainer found a new purpose straining stirred cocktails.

Sometimes I'll say a cocktail should be fine-strained, or double-strained. This means you'll need to pour your cocktail through a Hawthorne or Julep strainer, then through a fine-mesh sieve in order to catch small pieces of fruit pulp or herbs. For fine-straining, use a small, handheld sieve akin to a tea strainer.

MUDDLERS

Muddlers are used to crush soft fruits, extract essential oils from herbs and citrus peel, crack seeds and nuts and even crush ice (if you're feeling strong). When it comes to choosing a muddler the big question is: wood, plastic or steel? Wood is elegant and can take on most things, but it will need handwashing and drying. Plastic and steel work the same way, but are dishwasher friendly.

JUICER

If you're making cocktails, you're going to be squeezing plenty of citrus fruits. A lemon juicer will save you a lot of time and mess.

BLENDERS & FOOD PROCESSORS

For frozen cocktails, a blender is essential. When you're picking a blender, make sure you choose one that is big enough and packs enough power – at least 1000 watts. Blenders that promise they can crush ice and make smoothies are the best choice for cocktail making, as they're normally powerful and quick –

the faster the blade spins, the finer your ingredients will be processed. Although when it comes to making crushed ice, I tend to find food processors do a better job than blenders.

ICE CUBE TRAYS
You're going to need plenty of ice for your summer drinks. Buying bags of ice cubes and crushed ice is quick, easy and gives a great result. I pick up bags of ice from my local store for shaking and standard serves, then have fun making more interesting ice cubes if I want a particular look. Oversized ice cubes are great for shorter, spirit-forward drinks, like Old Fashioneds, while long, spear-shaped ice cubes can work in tall cocktails served in collins glasses. Making tiny ice cubes can look really cute in the glass and you can opt for cubes, spheres or even tiny hearts.

The Glass Cabinet

As the fashion for cocktails served in jam jars demonstrated, you don't need a fancy glass to serve your drinks, but sometimes it's nice to go all out. There are three basic glasses you need for your mixed drinks: a tall glass, a short glass and a glass with a stem. Use this guide to decide which one is right for you.

HIGHBALL & COLLINS GLASSES
Highball glasses are tall and skinny, while collins glasses are just tall. Collins glasses are typically a little bigger, but the difference between the two types is slight. Start off with a 350ml (12fl oz) glass, which should cover you for most tall drinks, then you can see if you need to supplement it with something bigger or smaller. This kind of glass is perfect for people who like long drinks, like Gin and Tonics or Moscow Mules, and they're also great for serving fruity Tiki cocktails and punches in.

ROCKS GLASSES

Lowball tumblers come in two basic sizes: single rock and double rock (aka the old fashioned glass). Single rock glasses are around 250–300ml (8½–10fl oz) and are ideal for things like Negronis. They comfortably fit a chunk of ice and your drink while still letting you slide a bar spoon around. Double rock glasses are 300–350ml (10–12fl oz) and while you can serve a whisky and soda in them, they also make great midsize glasses for drinks with crushed ice, like Juleps, Margaritas and Daisies.

COUPE, MARTINI & NICK & NORA GLASSES

Coupes, or champagne saucers, have wide bowls and are used for shaken or stirred cocktails that are served up (chilled, but without ice). Martini glasses are more angular – either v-shaped or bell-shaped – and are perfect for Martinis  (of course). Both coupes and martini glasses are usually around 200ml (7fl oz). A Nick & Nora glass is like a deeper, smaller coupe. They're usually around 120–160ml (4–6fl oz), so they're a little smaller. If you're keen on stirred drinks, like Manhattans, a set of Nick & Nora glasses might be for you. Otherwise, a coupe is a good all-rounder that'll work for shaken and stirred drinks, as well as Margaritas.

WINE, FLUTE & COPA GLASSES

Flutes for fizz and wine glasses for wine, obviously, but wine glasses are also good for spritzes and Gin and Tonics. Copa de balon glasses are Gin and Tonic glasses that evolved from red wine glasses in Spain. Their curved shape traps the gin's aroma, while  still letting it breathe, and leaves plenty of space for interesting garnishes. If you love an aromatic G&T and are a big fan of summer spritzes, a set of copa glasses is a good choice.

All the Right Moves

Like any activity that straddles the world of art and science, it's possible to get very nerdy about mixing drinks. Precise temperatures, optimum levels of dilution, how wet the ice is – every stage of cocktail-making is ripe for experimentation and rule-making (normally followed, fairly swiftly, by rule-breaking). As a committed amateur cocktail shaker, I stick with practical and simple methods when I'm mixing drinks at home and leave the high art of cocktail-making to the professionals. How granular you decide to get is up to you. This guide to the basic techniques will get you started. Once you have your foundation skills sorted, you can start to explore.

SHAKE OR STIR?

The fastest way to chill and blend a cocktail is to shake it, but not every cocktail should be shaken. This is because shaking foams them up, and they can end up looking cloudy, which isn't always the finish we want in a drink. A simple rule of thumb is that if your cocktail contains fruit, eggs or dairy, you shake it. If it's all booze, you stir it. As ever, there are exceptions to this rule, but broadly speaking it works for most cocktails.

HOW TO STIR

Stirred cocktails should be clear, crisp and have a silky texture. Start by chilling the mixing glass and the glass you're going to serve your cocktail in. Add enough ice to fill the mixing glass by half to two-thirds, pour in your ingredients and stir with a bar spoon. To hold a bar spoon effectively, place it between your thumb, index and middle fingers with the stem of the spoon resting between your index and middle finger. Place the spoon in the glass so it touches the base, then use your wrist to turn the spoon around the glass. The spoon will begin to spin between your fingers. Keep it moving and stir for at least 30 seconds before straining the cocktail into the chilled serving glass.

HOW TO SHAKE

Shaking a cocktail doesn't just chill, blend and dilute it, it also aerates it, and the air bubbles that are introduced give the drink texture. The first sip of a shaken cocktail should be lively and full of spark. When you're shaking cocktails, pour the ingredients into your shaker and then add ice. How much ice you add depends on how big the ice cubes are. A couple of really big ice cubes or a handful of smaller ones is usually enough. There is a theory that larger ice cubes create smaller bubbles, which gives you a finer texture, but the downside is you have to shake your drink for longer to chill and dilute it. Whatever size ice cubes you choose, once they're added all you need to do is seal your shaker (very important) and then shake well – 15–30 seconds should do it. Your shaker should feel cold and will often look frosty. Strain your cocktail into a chilled glass and serve.

DRY AND REVERSE DRY SHAKES

There are two extra ways to shake a cocktail if they have egg white in them: a dry shake and a reverse dry shake. The dry shake involves shaking all the cocktail ingredients together, including the egg white, until it foams, then adding ice and shaking again to chill the cocktail. A dry shake gives you smaller bubbles and a smoother foam.The reverse dry shake means you shake all the ingredients apart from the egg white together with ice, then strain out the cocktail, discard the ice and put the drink back into the shaker with the egg white. It gets shaken again to foam the egg white, then strained and served. With a reverse dry shake you get larger air bubbles in the egg white, which gives you a fluffier foam. Previously, I preferred reverse dry shaking, but these days I like the simplicity of dry shaking. It's up to you which one you prefer.

Simple Syrups & Fruit Purées

When you want to add instant flavour to your cocktails, reach for a jar of homemade syrup or fresh fruit purée. They're easy to make and will help you balance the aroma, acidity and sweetness in your mixed drinks.

SIMPLE SYRUPS

Simple syrups are liquid sweeteners that are typically made by boiling sugar and water together. They disperse sweetness evenly through drinks, so they're an essential part of your cocktail cabinet. The most basic syrup is made with white sugar, but you can experiment by using different sugars such as Demerara or palm sugar for a richer, fudgier flavour. Whatever sugar you opt for, use the same weight of sugar and water given in the recipe that follows. Swapping the sugar for honey will give you a lighter, more floral flavour, while infusing the syrup with herbs and spices is an easy way to add flavours to your mixed drinks.

SIMPLE SYRUP

Makes approximately 450ml (16fl oz)
250g (8¾oz) sugar
250ml (8½fl oz) water

Tip the sugar into a saucepan and pour in the water. Set the pan on a medium–high heat and bring to the boil, without stirring. Once boiling, set your timer for 2 minutes. After 2 minutes, take the pan off the heat and let the syrup cool. Transfer to a sterilized jar or tub, seal and store in the fridge for up to 1 month.

HONEY SYRUP

Makes approximately 450ml (16fl oz)
250ml (8½fl oz) water
250g (8¾oz) honey

Pour the water and honey into a pan and set it on a medium–high heat. Bring to the boil, without stirring. Once the pan is boiling, set your timer for 2 minutes. After 2 minutes, take the pan off the heat and let the syrup cool in the pan. Transfer the syrup to a sterilized jar or tub, seal and store in the fridge for up to 1 month.

FLAVOUR VARIATIONS

These infusions all follow the same method: make your simple syrup following the basic recipe, then take the pan off the heat, add your chosen flavouring and let the syrup steep for the suggested time. Strain through a fine-mesh sieve and store the syrup in a sterilized jar or tub, discarding the flavouring ingredient. They're ready to use straightaway, or you can store in the fridge for up to 1 month.

Hibiscus Syrup

Add 20g (¾oz) dried hibiscus flowers to the basic syrup and steep for 1–2 hours. Strain through a sieve into a bowl, pressing the flowers to squeeze out as much syrup as possible. The syrup should be a deep pink colour and have a tart, tangy flavour. The flowers will absorb a little of the syrup, so you will be left with approximately 400ml (14fl oz) syrup.
Used in Frozen Hibiscus Margarita (page 118)

Rose Syrup

Add 40g (1½oz) dried rose petals or buds to the syrup and steep for 1–2 hours.

Strain through a sieve into a bowl, pressing the flowers to squeeze out as much syrup as possible. The syrup should be pink with an aromatic, floral flavour. The flowers will absorb a little of the syrup, so you will be left with approximately 400ml (14fl oz) syrup.
Used in Rose & Cardamom Lassi (page 133)

Jalapeño Syrup

Slice 2 jalapeño chillies and add them to the syrup. Steep for 20 minutes, then taste to see if it has the right level of heat for you. If you'd like it a little hotter, steep for another 10 minutes. For a milder syrup, don't slice the chillies. Instead, steep them whole in the syrup for 30 minutes to extract the chillies' flavour without the heat.
Used in Spicy Watermelon & Lime Frosé (page 102) and Bloody Maria (page 98)

Mint Syrup

Add 20g (¾oz) fresh mint sprigs to the syrup and steep for 1–2 hours. The syrup should be pale green and have a fresh, minty flavour.
Used in Limonana (page 129)

Rhubarb Syrup

Trim 250g (8¾oz) rhubarb and chop it into bite-sized chunks. Add to the syrup and steep for 1–2 hours. Lift the rhubarb out with a slotted spoon and transfer to a tub – the rhubarb will keep for 2–3 days in the fridge and is delicious served with yogurt and granola for breakfast. The syrup should have a pale pink colour and a tart flavour. The rhubarb will absorb some of the syrup, so you will be left with approximately 300ml (10fl oz) syrup.

Used in Rhubarb & Red Vermouth Spritz (page 74), Rhubarb & Vanilla Ice Cream Float (page 46) and Rhubarb & Lemongrass Fizz (page 117)

FRESH FRUIT PURÉES

Summer drinks demand fresh fruit, but adding chunks of fruit to your shaker can muddy the colour, finish and texture of your cocktail without imparting enough of the fruit's flavour. The solution? Use a purée. They have a silky consistency and disperse easily through your drink, making sure every mouthful captures the essence of your favourite fruit. You can purée pretty much any fruit, but these are the ones I've used in this book and which taste most like summer to me.

Peach
Makes 250ml (8½fl oz)

Slice a small cross in the base of 4 ripe peaches, weighing approximately 500g (17¾oz). Place them in a heatproof bowl. Boil a kettle of water and pour it over the peaches to cover them. Set aside for 20 minutes, then drain. Gently pull the skin away from the peaches and discard. Halve the peaches and scoop out the stones. Pop the peaches back into the bowl and use a handheld stick blender to blitz them into a smooth purée. You can press it through a fine-mesh sieve for an even silkier texture, if you like. Scoop into a sterilized jar and store in the fridge for up to 1 week.

Used in Bellitini (page 58), Bourbon & Peach Smash (page 77) and Porch Punch (page 94)

Strawberry
Makes 275ml (9fl oz)

Rinse 450g (16oz) strawberries and hull them – removing the green tops and white

middle. Place in a bowl and use a handheld stick blender to blitz them into a smooth purée. Scoop into a fine-mesh sieve set over a clean bowl and press with a wooden spoon to push the smooth purée through the sieve, leaving any seeds behind. Scoop the purée into a sterilized jar and store in the fridge for up to 1 week.
Used in Strawberries & Cream Martini (page 78), Rossini (page 45) and Strawberry Milk Bubble Tea (page 29)

Raspberry
Makes 300ml (10fl oz)

Rinse 450g (16oz) raspberries. Place in a bowl and use a handheld stick blender to blitz them into a smooth purée. Scoop into a fine-mesh sieve set over a clean bowl and press with a wooden spoon to push the purée through the sieve, leaving any seeds behind. Scoop the purée into a sterilized jar and store in the fridge for up to 1 week.
Used in Raspberry & Basil Cream Soda (page 41) and Raspberry Ramble (page 54)

Cantaloupe Melon Juice
Makes 300ml (10fl oz)

Halve 1 cantaloupe melon, weighing approximately 1kg (35oz), and scoop out the seeds. Slice the skin away from the flesh. If you have a juicer, feed the melon through that to extract the juice. If not, pop the melon into a food processor or blender and blitz until you have a finely chopped purée. Scoop into a sieve and press the pulp to extract as much

STERILIZING JARS AND BOTTLES

To sterilize glass jars and bottles, preheat your oven to 160°C/Fan 140°C/320°F/ Gas Mark 3. Wash the jars and/or bottles in hot soapy water (including the lids for the jars, if they have them), then rinse and place on a baking tray. Slide into the oven and heat for around 15 minutes. Take them out of the oven and let them cool until they're cold enough to handle, then add the syrup or purée and seal.

juice as possible. If you can, leave it for a few hours to let the juice drip through. Transfer to a sterilized jar or bottle and seal. The juice will keep in the fridge for up to 3 days.

The melon pulp is edible. Keep it in a tub in the fridge, ripple it through yogurt and serve with granola for breakfast. *Used in White Sangria (page 110)*

Make Your Own Soft Drinks

There are several soft drinks used in this book, but nothing is quite as satisfying as a glass of homemade lemonade. Sweet and tangy, lemonade is a tasty mix of fresh citrus juice, simple syrup and water. I normally make it with still tap water, but you can swap in sparkling water if you like your lemonade with a little fizz. If you prefer a tangier soft drink, try making a Spiced Pineapple Shrub; 'fruit vinegars' have been a popular non-alcoholic option for hundreds of years and this recipe has a touch of spice to warm up the shrub's bright flavour. Delicious by itself, you can also use it to make cocktails including the Nolada (page 38) and the Bird of Paradise (page 34).

HOMEMADE LEMONADE
Makes approximately 1.15 ltrs (39fl oz)
120ml (4fl oz) fresh lemon juice
50ml (1¾fl oz) fresh orange juice
225ml (7½fl oz) Simple Syrup (see page 13)
750ml (25¼fl oz) cold water
Lemon slices, to garnish

Pour the lemon juice, orange juice, Simple Syrup and water into a large pitcher. Add a few handfuls of ice and stir to mix. Tuck a few fresh lemon slices into the pitcher and serve straightaway.

FLAVOUR VARIATIONS
Limeade
Use 120ml (4fl oz) fresh lime juice and 50ml (1¾fl oz) fresh lemon juice in place of the lemon and orange juice.

17

Grapefruitade

Use 200ml (7fl oz) fresh grapefruit juice and 90ml (3fl oz) fresh lime juice in place of the lemon and orange juice.

Rhubarb Lemonade

Swap Rhubarb Simple Syrup (see page 15) for the basic Simple Syrup.

Rose Lemonade

Swap Rose Simple Syrup (see page 14) for the basic Simple Syrup.

Hibiscus Lemonade

Swap Hibiscus Simple Syrup (see page 14) for the basic Simple Syrup.

SPICED PINEAPPLE SHRUB

Makes 450ml (16fl oz)

1 pineapple, weighing
    approximately 1.2kg (42oz)
30g (1oz) fresh ginger
200g (7oz) white sugar
200ml (7fl oz) cold water
1 cinnamon stick
1 star anise
4 whole cloves
200ml (7fl oz) apple cider
    vinegar

Trim the top and base off the pineapple, then use a sharp knife to slice off the skin. Use the tip of the knife to slice out any woody eyes left in the pineapple. Quarter it lengthways, then roughly chop it. You should have around 500g (17¾oz).

Slice the chunk of ginger (no need to peel it). Tip the sugar into a large pan and pour in the water. Set on a medium heat until the sugar dissolves, stirring occasionally. Add the pineapple with the ginger, cinnamon, star anise and cloves. Bring to a gentle simmer. Pop on a lid and simmer for 15–20 minutes until the pineapple chunks are soft.

Pour in the vinegar and bring back to a simmer. Take the pan off the heat and let it cool for 1–2 hours, then strain the liquid into a jug through a fine-mesh sieve. Press with a wooden spoon to squeeze out as much juice as possible. Discard the pineapple pulp and spices. Pour the shrub into a sterilized bottle or jar, let it cool, then store in the fridge. The shrub will keep for up to 2 months. To serve as a soft drink, mix 30–50ml (1–1¾fl oz) Spiced Pineapple Shrub with sparkling water and serve over ice.

The Recipes

Note: All recipes serve 1, unless otherwise stated

First Word

One of the 20th-century's classic cocktails, The Last Word was invented at the Detroit Athletics Club around 1916. A mix of gin, green chartreuse, maraschino and lime juice, it's a tangy and sprightly cocktail that managed to survive Prohibition and was still on bar menus well into the 1950s. Like many cocktails of that era, though, it fell out of fashion and was in danger of becoming a forgotten relic. But, luckily for both the cocktail and us, bartender Murray Stenson picked up a 1950s cocktail book, rediscovered the recipe and put it on the menu at the Zig Zag Café in Seattle in 2003. The Last Word was a hit again, and the craft cocktail boom of the 2000s saw many riffs and variations on the drink. This version swaps the maraschino for elderflower liqueur, which adds a subtly floral flavour to the drink. Elderflower trees blossom in early May, when their delicate, talcum-powder scent drifts across parks and gardens, signalling that summer is on its way. I always associate elderflower with the start of the sunny season, which is why this version of the cocktail is the First Word rather than the last.

20ml (¾fl oz) London dry gin
20ml (¾fl oz) green chartreuse
20ml (¾fl oz) elderflower liqueur
20ml (¾fl oz) fresh lime juice
Maraschino cherry, to garnish

INSTRUCTIONS

Place a small martini or coupe glass in the freezer for 5–10 minutes to chill, or fill with ice and set aside to chill. Add a cupful of ice to a cocktail shaker. Pour in the gin, green chartreuse, elderflower liqueur and fresh lime juice. Seal the shaker and shake vigorously for 30 seconds or so until chilled. Empty any ice out of the glass. Strain in the First Word mix and drop in a maraschino cherry to garnish.

Mint Julep

The Mint Julep is synonymous with America's Deep South. It's especially associated with the Kentucky Derby, a horse race run every May at Churchill Downs in Louisville. The Mint Julep has been the Derby's official drink since the 1930s; Churchill Downs estimate they sell over 120,000 Mint Juleps during the Derby. Mint Juleps have been made in the USA since the early 19th century and, like any old and venerable drink, there's a lot of debate over the right way to make it. The main area of contention is whether to shake the cocktail or churn it. Ever the peacemaker, I like to do both. Shaking the mint, bourbon and Simple Syrup together provides an initial chill and ensures the mint's fragrance is infused into the drink. Churning the mix in the glass (or julep tin, if you have one) helps to dilute it a little, creating a long drink that perfectly balances the bourbon's warmth with the freshness of the mint. It's a fire and ice combo that will cool you down on the hottest of summer days.

8 fresh mint leaves
60ml (2fl oz) bourbon
10ml (¼fl oz) Simple Syrup (see page 13)
2 dashes of Angostura bitters
Mint sprig, to garnish

INSTRUCTIONS

Place the mint leaves in a cocktail shaker and use a muddler or the end of a wooden spoon to bruise them so you can just smell their fragrance. Pour in the bourbon and Simple Syrup. Dash in the Angostura bitters and add a cupful of ice. Seal and shake vigorously for 30 seconds or until well chilled. Fill a julep tin or old fashioned glass with crushed ice. Fine-strain in the Mint Julep mix. Use a bar spoon to churn the ice and Julep for around 30 seconds–1 minute, then top up the crushed ice and churn again. Top up the crushed ice one last time and tuck in a mint sprig to garnish. Serve with reusable straws.

Mocha Hard Shake

The first iced coffee of the year is a special moment. It means that summer has definitely arrived and it's time to dig out my flip flops, beach towel and suntan cream. For a few months I'll skip my morning flat white and swap it for an iced latte. On the weekends, this Mocha Hard Shake is a brunch-time treat. It's made with cold brewed coffee that's steeped overnight to gently extract the flavour from the beans while leaving behind the bitterness (see the box below for tips on how to make the perfect cup of cold brew). The combination of white and dark crème de cacao gives the cocktail a chocolatey flavour, while whizzing them with the milk in a blender creates a foam that your local barista would be proud of. The two chocolate liqueurs are quite sweet, so I've suggested serving Simple Syrup (or honey or maple syrup) on the side, so your guests can sweeten their coffee to suit their own palates. This also gives you the option to use flavoured syrup, like salted caramel, vanilla cinnamon or hazelnut. Put a shaker filled with cinnamon or cocoa powder on the table and you've practically set up your own brew bar at home.

Serves 6

120ml (4fl oz) dark crème de cacao
120ml (4fl oz) white crème de cacao
250ml (8½fl oz) full-fat (full-cream) milk
1 litre (1¾ pints) cold-brew coffee (see box)
Simple Syrup, to serve (see page 13)

INSTRUCTIONS

Pour the dark crème de cacao, white crème de cacao and milk into a blender. Whizz for 1–2 minutes until combined and frothy. Fill 6 collins glasses with ice and pour in the cold-brew coffee. Top up each glass with the boozy milk mixture. Serve with reusable straws and Simple Syrup on the side.

HOW TO MAKE COLD-BREW COFFEE

There are two ways to brew a good cup of coffee: quickly, using heat and pressure, or slowly, using time to gently extract the flavour from the beans while leaving their bitterness behind. Cold-brewing coffee follows the latter method. A simple ratio for making a cup of cold-brew coffee is to steep 1 tablespoon of filter coffee grounds in 300ml (10fl oz) cold water for 12 hours. Strain it through a fine-mesh sieve lined with a coffee filter. Serve it straight up, over ice or with a splash of milk or cream. If you want to sweeten it, use a liquid sweetener like Simple Syrup, honey or maple syrup. You can use this ratio to make big batches of cold brew. It'll keep in a sealed jar or bottle in the fridge for up to two weeks, so you can always have some coffee on hand for cocktails like this Hard Shake or ready to serve with breakfast on warm, sunny days.

Cucumber & Lime Margarita

Are Margaritas the perfect poolside drink? Possibly. Do you need to be lounging by a pool under a sun-streaked, azure sky while a DJ plays summer beats and palm trees sway in the breeze in order to enjoy a Marg? It helps, but it's not essential. Especially when you can recreate the vibes of an LA rooftop bar in your own back garden, on your balcony or just in your kitchen by mixing up a batch of these Cucumber & Lime Margaritas. Adding cucumber into the mix doesn't just make this drink extra refreshing, it also makes it smoother. The fresh, grassy flavour rounds out the lime's zing, and adds a cooling juiciness to the drink. If you're looking to chill this summer, make sure you add cucumber to your Margarita mix.

Serves 2

1 cucumber, weighing approximately 300g (10½oz)
100ml (3½fl oz) fresh lime juice
1 lime wedge
2 tsp fine sea salt and a pinch of chilli powder,
    to decorate the glasses
90ml (3fl oz) silver tequila
60ml (2fl oz) triple sec
30ml (1fl oz) agave nectar
6 dashes of cucumber bitters
2 lime wheels, to garnish

continued **»**

INSTRUCTIONS

Roughly chop the cucumber and place in a blender. Pour in the lime juice and blend again until smooth and combined. Set a fine-mesh sieve over a bowl and pour in the cucumber and lime mix. Push the purée through the sieve to extract as much juice as possible, leaving behind the dry pulp. Discard the pulp. You should have around 300ml (10fl oz) cucumber and lime juice.

Rub the rim of 2 old fashioned glasses with a lime wedge to dampen them. Shake a few teaspoons of fine sea salt onto a plate and stir in a pinch of chilli powder. Dip the glass rims into the chilli salt to lightly coat. Set aside.

Measure out 60ml (2fl oz) of the lime and cucumber juice into a cocktail shaker, reserving the rest (see box below). Add the silver tequila, triple sec and agave nectar with a generous handful of ice. Dash in the cucumber bitters. Seal the shaker and shake vigorously for 30 seconds or so until chilled. Add fresh ice to the glasses and strain in the Margarita mix. Garnish each glass with a lime wheel.

USING UP YOUR JUICE MIX

You'll need 60ml (2fl oz) of the lime and cucumber mix to make 2 Margaritas following this recipe. The rest can be stored in the fridge for up to 3 days, ready to make more Margaritas – it also freezes really well. Pour into ice cube trays to freeze, then transfer to a freezerproof bag or tub. Defrost the cucumber and lime ice cubes to make the Margaritas following this recipe, or add the frozen cubes to a blender with the tequila, triple sec and agave nectar, along with a cupful of plain ice, and blitz to make frozen Cucumber & Lime Margaritas.

Strawberry Milk Bubble Tea

Bubble tea – aka boba – is a bona-fide, 21st-century drink sensation. An iced milky tea with a layer of gelatinous tapioca pearls, it's a relatively recent invention that has quickly become established in major cities all around the world. Boba culture originated in Taiwan in the 1980s. According to one origin story, Taiwanese entrepreneur Tu Tsong He was inspired by the tapioca desserts in the market near his tea shop, and created a pearl green tea drink with white tapioca pearls that was an immediate hit. An alternative claim comes from Lin Hsiu Hui, who was a product manager at a teashop chain. At a staff meeting she tipped a tapioca dessert into her cup of tea. Her colleagues loved it and put it on the menu straight away. The two claimants went to court to try to settle who first invented bubble tea and had the right to sell it. Luckily for us, the Taiwanese justice system decided bubble tea was a drink anyone could make and boba shops began opening up across the globe. When you're making it at home, check the cooking instructions on your tapioca pearls. Lots of tapioca pearls are quick-cook, but there are some brands that take up to 30 minutes. Make sure you know which one you've got so you can simmer your tapioca to get that perfect, chewy texture.

Serves 2

100g (3½oz) black sugar tapioca pearls
2 tbsp black tea leaves or 2 tea bags
120ml (4fl oz) fresh strawberry purée
600ml (20fl oz) full-fat (full-cream) milk, chilled
30ml (1fl oz) Simple Syrup (see page 13)

continued **》**

INSTRUCTIONS

Bring 1 litre (1¾ pints) hot water to the boil in a medium-sized saucepan. When the water is boiling, slowly shake in the tapioca pearls. Bring the water back to the boil. Let the pearls come to the surface of the water, then turn the heat down a little and pop on a lid. Simmer for 5 minutes. Lift the pearls out of the water with a slotted spoon and transfer them to a bowl of cold water to cool them. While the tapioca pearls simmer, place the tea in a heatproof pitcher. Fill your kettle and boil it. Cover the tea with 150ml (5¼fl oz) freshly boiled water. Set aside to steep for 4–8 minutes, depending on how strong you would like your tea. Strain and set aside until you're ready to make your milk tea. Stir the strawberry purée, milk and Simple Syrup together in a pitcher. To assemble your bubble teas, drain the tapioca pearls and add them to 2 bubble teacups or collins glasses. Pour in the tea, then top up with the strawberry milk and stir to mix. Add a handful of ice to each glass and serve with reusable straws.

Vivi

My editor, Caitlin Doyle, passed the recipe for this zingy thirst-quencher to me just after we heard that *Summer Sparklers* had been given the go-ahead. Her colleague, Jay C Luck, had sent her the recipe because he thought it would be perfect for the book. Having tried it, I have to agree. Jay created this cocktail during the heatwave of 2022, when cold drinks were in high demand. I say Jay created it, but he did have some help from his daughter Vivienne, who's been mixing mocktails since she was little. Under Vivi's expert guidance, Jay came up with a tall summer drink that's simple to mix, not too boozy and not too sugary. The double dose of citrus, thanks to the fresh lime juice and the Mexican lime soda, keeps the flavours crisp and sharp. Jay named this cocktail after Vivi, but if you want to try one of Vivi's own recipes, turn to page 61, where you'll find her alcohol-free Ibiza Sunset.

35ml (1¼fl oz) reposado tequila
15ml (½fl oz) fresh lime juice
120ml (4fl oz) Mexican lime soda, chilled
Lime wedge, to garnish

INSTRUCTIONS

Fill a highball glass with ice. Pour in the tequila and fresh lime juice. Top up with the chilled Mexican lime soda and gently stir to mix. Squeeze a lime wedge over the top, then drop it into the glass.

Bird of Paradise

The perfect summer cocktail is good for sipping – long enough that you can take a thirst-quenching gulp without burning the back of your throat with the alcohol or having it go straight to your head. It's crisp enough to be refreshing, and a little sweet but not so sugary that it tastes like a melted lolly. This pale-pink drink meets all those criteria, making it a sunny-season essential. A lot of the cocktail's flavour comes from the Spiced Pineapple Shrub (see page 18), which balances pineapple's tropical juiciness with a sharp dash of vinegar and a warming pinch of spice. It gives this citrus-forward cocktail an interesting base note that's brightened by the grenadine and given heft by the heat of the rum. If you don't want to make your own pineapple shrub, you can swap it for pineapple juice. The cocktail will be sweeter, but just as perfect for lingering over on hot days and warm nights.

50ml (1¾fl oz) light rum
25ml (¾fl oz) Spiced Pineapple Shrub (see page 18)
25ml (¾fl oz) fresh lime juice
15ml (½fl oz) grenadine syrup
15ml (½fl oz) fresh egg white
Maraschino cherry and lime wheel, to garnish

INSTRUCTIONS

Half-fill a cocktail shaker with ice, then pour in all the ingredients except the egg white. Seal and shake well for around 30 seconds or until well chilled. Strain into a glass (not your serving glass) and discard the ice from the shaker. Pour the chilled cocktail mix back into the shaker, add the egg white, seal and shake well for another 30 seconds or until it feels and sounds light – dry shaking the cocktail like this will help the egg white foam up, forming a fluffy topping for your cocktail. Fill an old fashioned glass with ice and pour in the Bird of Paradise mix. Thread a maraschino cherry and lime wheel onto a cocktail pick and rest it on the glass to garnish.

Spritz Veneziano

Spritz Veneziano, Spritz al Bitter, Aperol Spritz or simply just Spritz – whatever you call this drink, there's no denying that it's the daddy of all the Italian spritzes. It's the original aperitivo. The drink has its origins in the late 19th century, when the Veneto region of Italy was still part of the Austro-Hungarian empire. Austrian soldiers found Italian wines too strong, so they diluted them with a splash of soda water – *spritz* is German for 'splash'. Over time the drink evolved, with the Italians adding a bit more booze back in, until we've ended up with the spritz we know and love today. There is a range of bitter Italian liqueurs you can use to make your spritz. Aperol is the sweetest and most easy drinking, but if you'd like to go a little more bitter, try Campari, while Cynar, Amaro Averna or Cocchi Americano all bring a more stringent, herbal flavour to the spritz. Whichever bitter you choose to make your spritz with, stick to the 3:2:1 formula (3 parts prosecco, 2 parts bitter, 1 part soda) and you can't go wrong.

60ml (2fl oz) Aperol
90ml (3fl oz) dry prosecco, chilled
30ml (1fl oz) soda water, chilled
Orange wheel and a green olive, to garnish

INSTRUCTIONS

Fill a wine glass or copa glass with ice. Pour in the Aperol and top up the glass with the chilled prosecco. Stir to mix, then top up the glass with the chilled soda water. Give it a quick stir to just mix the drink. Thread an orange wheel and an olive onto a cocktail pick, then drop it into the glass.

Nolada

This zero-proof riff on the Piña Colada has all the flavour of that classic beach drink, but it's lighter on both the calories and the rum. A lot of this drink's appeal comes from the Spiced Pineapple Shrub (see page 18); it combines the sweetness of pineapple with a tang of vinegar, giving it an acidic kick that's guaranteed to make your mouth water. Coconut water adds a subtle tropical flavour, while the squeeze of fresh lime juice brings all the ingredients together. In cocktails, small quantities of citrus juices often act in the same way salt does in meals – heightening the flavours and making them bloom. So even though it's only a little splash of lime juice, don't skip it. If you do want to make this mocktail boozy, add a shot of light rum. (See page 138 for a classic rum, pineapple and coconut Piña Colada.)

60ml (2fl oz) Spiced Pineapple Shrub (see page 18)
90ml (3fl oz) coconut water
10ml (¼fl oz) fresh lime juice
Lime wedge, to garnish

INSTRUCTIONS
Fill a collins glass with ice. Pour in the Pineapple Shrub, coconut water and lime juice. Stir to mix, then garnish with a lime wedge.

Raspberry & Basil Cream Soda

Do you dream of soda fountains and pastel-pink ice cream parlours? Then this zero-proof cocktail is the drink for you. It's inspired by American cream sodas, the fizzy drinks that taste like melted ice cream and make me think of Jimmy Stewart movies. This fresh-fruit version swaps the traditional vanilla flavouring in favour of real cream stirred with soda water and floated on top of a luscious layer of fresh raspberry purée (see page 16). If you're not keen on basil, you can swap it for a few fresh mint leaves or thyme sprigs, or leave out the herbs entirely and just enjoy the combination of sweet red raspberries and rich dairy cream.

4 fresh basil leaves
30ml (1fl oz) fresh raspberry purée
25ml (¾fl oz) Simple Syrup (see page 13)
100ml (3½fl oz) soda water, chilled
25ml (¾fl oz) single cream (light cream)
Fresh raspberries, to garnish

INSTRUCTIONS

Place the basil leaves in a highball glass and use a muddler or the end of a wooden spoon to bash them a few times until they're bruised and aromatic. Pour in the raspberry purée and Simple Syrup and stir to mix. Fill the glass with ice, then pour in the chilled soda water and stir to mix. Pour the cream into the glass, then gently stir to ripple the cream through the soda. Drop in a couple of raspberries to garnish and serve with reusable straws.

Pimm's No 1 Spritz

James Pimm owned an oyster bar in London and he wanted a
tonic wine to serve alongside his oysters as an aid to digestion,
but he couldn't find the right drink among the brewhouses
and distilleries of 19th-century London. So he got to mixing
and, in 1823, he invented Pimm's No 1. He based his fruity drink
on gin, blending it with a secret combination of herbs, spices
and liqueurs. It went down well with Pimm's oyster platters and,
although we don't think of it as a natural pairing with seafood
today, we do reach for it whenever the sun starts to shine.
It's a drink that's inextricably linked with summer in England,
especially when it's mixed with lemonade to make a Pimm's Cup
(see page 90). This single-serve twist on the traditional punch
swaps the lemonade for something a bit more glamorous –
dry sparkling wine. In keeping with the English vibe, you could
use a citrusy English sparkling wine as the mixer. If English
fizz hasn't made it to your local bottle shop, use champagne,
crémant de Limoux, cava or Tasmanian sparkling wine.

45ml (1½fl oz) Pimm's No 1 Cup
15ml (½fl oz) triple sec
60ml (2fl oz) dry sparkling wine, chilled
90ml (3fl oz) ginger ale, chilled
Cucumber ribbon and orange twist, to garnish

INSTRUCTIONS
Half-fill a wine glass with ice. Pour in the Pimm's and triple sec
and stir to mix. Top up the glass with the chilled sparkling wine
and ginger ale, then gently stir again. Thread a cucumber ribbon
onto a cocktail pick and drop it into the glass. Garnish with an
orange twist.

Rossini

The Bellini might be Italy's most famous fruit 'n' fizz cocktail (and the inspiration for the Bellitini in this book, on page 58) but it's not the only fruity prosecco cocktail to have been invented in Southern Europe, there's also the Rossini. Like the Bellini, it was invented in Venice in the mid-20th century. In fact, it was created in the same bar in which the Bellini was first mixed, and was developed by the barman who was responsible for the Bellini – Giuseppe Cipriani. To be honest, he was probably just doing a riff on his original drink, but what a riff it is. Fresh strawberry purée (see page 15) with a little bump of crème de fraise add richness to the crisp floral flavour of dry prosecco. It's a very elegant drink, and obviously it's perfect for parties. To save time, mix the strawberry purée and crème de fraise together a few hours before the party and chill in the fridge. Then they're ready to be added to glasses and topped up with fizz as soon as your guests arrive.

Serves 6
150ml (5¼fl oz) fresh strawberry purée
90ml (3fl oz) crème de fraise
30ml (1fl oz) fresh lemon juice
600ml (20fl oz) dry prosecco, chilled
Strawberries, to garnish

INSTRUCTIONS
In a small pitcher, combine the strawberry purée, crème de fraise and lemon juice. Chill this until you're ready to pour the Rossinis – ideally at least for 1 hour. You can make this the day before and store in the fridge. To make the Rossinis, pour the strawberry mix into 6 flute glasses. Top up with the chilled prosecco and gently stir to mix. Garnish each glass with a small strawberry and serve.

Rhubarb & Vanilla Ice Cream Float

Rhubarb with vanilla makes a classic combination, as delicious in a pie or crumble as in this non-alcoholic drink. Ice cream floats are a childhood favourite, making this mocktail either a nostalgic trip down memory lane or – if this drink is being made for you – an introduction to the magic of ice cream sodas. Part of the pleasure is the way the soda foams up as soon as it hits the ice cream, forming a bubbly froth that's as light and fluffy as a cloud. The reaction is instant and the foam will fill your glass, so don't pour in the soda too enthusiastically – you need to steadily build a layer of foam rather than a fizzing lather. Once you've mastered the art of the ice cream float serve, you can use these measurements to make all sorts of floats, picking from your favourite flavour combinations. Raspberry syrup and vanilla ice cream, mint syrup and chocolate ice cream, or rose syrup and strawberry ice cream are all fab float mixes.

Serves 4

8 scoops of vanilla ice cream
240ml (8fl oz) rhubarb syrup
750ml (1.3 pints) cream soda, chilled

INSTRUCTIONS

Place 2 scoops of vanilla ice cream into each of the 4 collins glasses. Pour 60ml (2fl oz) rhubarb syrup into each glass, then top up with the chilled cream soda. You'll need to tilt the glasses as you pour, so you're pouring the cream soda down the side of the glass rather than directly onto the ice cream. The soda will foam up, so do this slowly. You may need to half-fill each glass with soda, then let the bubbles die down before topping them up. Serve the ice cream sodas straight away with reusable straws, so you can stir the cordial, ice cream and soda together in the glass.

Gin Daisy

Daisies and Margaritas are sister cocktails. The Daisy was invented first; it was a popular cocktail in the 1920s and 1930s. At its most basic, it was a spirit shaken with a liqueur (often orange) and citrus juice. You could order Gin Daisies, Brandy Daisies, Vodka Daisies and, eventually, Tequila Daisies. The Tequila Daisy cast a spell on barkeeps, who kept tweaking and refining the mix until we ended up with Margaritas (margarita means 'daisy' in Spanish). The other Daisies were kind of forgotten – kind of, but not quite. You'll still find Daisies on the occasional bar menu, and here, in this book. This Gin Daisy is a lively long drink that's very gin forward. Use a London dry gin when you're mixing it, as the punchy juniper flavour will blend beautifully with the orange triple sec, lime juice and tangy, pomegranate-flavoured syrup.

50ml (1¾fl oz) London dry gin
8ml (¼fl oz) triple sec
8ml (¼fl oz) fresh lemon juice
8ml (¼fl oz) grenadine syrup
Dash of soda water, chilled
Maraschino cherry, to garnish

INSTRUCTIONS

Half-fill a cocktail shaker with ice, then pour in all the ingredients except the soda water. Seal and shake well for around 30 seconds or until well chilled. Fill an old fashioned glass with crushed ice and strain in the Gin Daisy. Top up with a dash of chilled soda water, then drop in a maraschino cherry to garnish.

Cherry Negroni

If you've ever tried a Negroni and found it just a little too punchy, this take on the famous Italian aperitivo could be for you. Traditionally, a Negroni is made with gin, Campari and sweet vermouth, which makes for a very boozy and very bitter drink. It's something that cocktail fans tend to learn to love rather than embrace as their favourite straight away. If you like the idea of a Negroni but you struggle with the drink's booze-forward bitterness, try easing yourself in with this smooth variation on the formula. It's made with maraschino instead of gin, which is a type of sweet cherry liqueur that's typically lower in alcohol than gin. The liqueur's stickiness knocks off some of the rough edges of the Campari, and its lower ABV means there's less burn from the alcohol, making this a more approachable way to enjoy this style of drink.

25ml (¾fl oz) maraschino
25ml (¾fl oz) Campari
25ml (¾fl oz) sweet vermouth
Orange wheel and maraschino cherry, to garnish

INSTRUCTIONS

Fill an old fashioned glass with ice. Pour in the maraschino, Campari and sweet vermouth. Stir well to chill. Thread an orange wheel and maraschino cherry onto a cocktail pick and drop into the glass to garnish.

Dear Eli,
Italy is a dream.
Wish you were
here!

— K

Eli McKenna
1028 Main St.
Philadelphia, PA
19101
U.S.A.

White Russian Affogato

This tipsy take on a popular Italian sweet means you can have your dessert and drink it, too. Affogato means 'drowned' and normally it's a scoop of vanilla ice cream that's being drowned by fresh, hot espresso. I've added a couple of ingredients from a White Russian cocktail to create a dessert that's halfway to being a hard shake. If you let the ice cream melt, you'll end up with a rich and creamy drink, but I think half the fun is scooping up spoonfuls of cold ice cream and swirling them in the warm coffee, vanilla vodka and coffee liqueur before taking a bite, so each mouthful is a mixture of hot, cold and fierce.

2 scoops of vanilla ice cream
25ml (¾fl oz) vanilla vodka
25ml (¾fl oz) coffee liqueur
15ml (½fl oz) Simple Syrup (see page 13)
45ml (1½fl oz) freshly made espresso

INSTRUCTIONS
Add 2 scoops of vanilla ice cream to a rocks glass, then pour over the vanilla vodka, coffee liqueur and Simple Syrup. Pour over the hot espresso and serve straight away, with a teaspoon to stir and scoop up the ice cream.

Raspberry Ramble

This berry-sweet cocktail is a twist on the Bramble, a classic cocktail invented in the 1980s by legendary mixed drink maestro Dick Bradsell. He invented the cocktail while working at Fred's Bar in Soho, London, inspired by the country walks he used to take on the Isle of Wight as a child. On those strolls, he would get scratched by bramble bushes – especially when he was picking blackberries off the bushes. When he wanted to create a cocktail that was quintessentially British, he remembered those thorny hedgerows and created a gin-based cocktail that was topped with a sticky swirl of crème de mûre. This riff on Bradsell's original swaps the blackberries for raspberries, and it takes its inspiration from a childhood memory of my own – bowls of raspberry ripple ice cream. The base layer of the cocktail is a vanilla vodka sour, while the top combines crème de framboise with homemade raspberry purée (see page 16). Together they taste like a sumptuous iced dessert.

60ml (2fl oz) vanilla vodka
30ml (1fl oz) fresh lime juice
15ml (½fl oz) Simple Syrup (see page 13)
15ml (½fl oz) crème de framboise
30ml (1fl oz) raspberry purée
Raspberries and lime slice, to garnish

INSTRUCTIONS

Fill an old fashioned glass with crushed ice. Pour the vodka, lime juice and Simple Syrup over the ice, then gently stir together. Top up the crushed ice so it fills the glass again. In a separate glass, stir the crème de framboise and raspberry purée together until smooth and combined, then pour over the top of the drink so it stains the ice. Top with a couple of raspberries and a lime slice. Serve with 2 short, reusable straws.

Jacqueline

At summer *ferias* in Southern France, revellers – known as *festayre* – keep themselves cool with tall glasses of this cherry-red cocktail. The festivals are traditionally held to celebrate saints' days or harvests, and they take place over a couple of days. Red-and-white-clad partygoers gather in town squares and hop between bars and cafés, where they celebrate with drinks that are a little buzzy but not too boozy. The Jacqueline fits the bill perfectly. Also called a Jaja, it's an apéritif that perks up dry white wine by mixing in a dash of fruity grenadine syrup and then adds a little lemonade sparkle. It's best made with a wine that has a good dose of acidity to match the grenadine's sweetness, like an unoaked sauvignon blanc or a chenin blanc. It's a great drink for turning an everyday white wine into something special.

15ml (½fl oz) grenadine syrup
80ml (2¾fl oz) dry white wine, chilled
40ml (1½fl oz) sparkling lemonade
Lemon slice, to garnish

INSTRUCTIONS

Fill a highball glass with ice. Pour in the grenadine syrup and white wine and gently stir to mix. Top up the ice again, if necessary. Pour in the sparkling lemonade to top up the glass. Garnish with a lemon slice.

Bellitini

This fresh-fruit martini was inspired by the Bellini, the
white peach and prosecco cocktail that's served in bars all
over Venice. I wanted to capture both the stone-fruit flavour
and the glamour of that drink in a cocktail that was shorter
and a little more booze forward. Enter the Martini. Using a
fresh peach purée is essential in this drink (see page 15).
If you can get your hands on Italian white peaches when
they're in season, use those, but regular peaches will work
perfectly, too. Normally I'd fine-strain a cocktail made
with fresh fruit, but if you sieved your peach purée when
you made it (time consuming, but worth it), then you don't
need to double-strain the mix when you pour it out of the
shaker. The purée gives the cocktail a slinky, silky texture that
feels incredibly luxurious. The Bellitini will elevate any event,
whether it's drinks with friends, dinner à deux or just a night
in binge-watching box sets.

3 tbsp peach purée
50ml (1¾fl oz) vodka
25ml (¾fl oz) crème de pêche liqueur
15ml (½fl oz) Simple Syrup (see page 13)
8ml (¼fl oz) fresh lemon juice
3 dashes of peach bitters
Lemon twist, to garnish

INSTRUCTIONS

Place a martini glass in the freezer for 5–10 minutes to chill, or fill
it with ice and set aside to chill. Half-fill a cocktail shaker with ice.
Add the peach purée, then pour in the vodka, crème de pêche
liqueur, Simple Syrup and lemon juice. Add the dashes of peach
bitters, then seal the shaker and shake vigorously for 30 seconds
or so until well chilled. Empty any ice out of the martini glass,
then strain in the Bellitini and garnish with a lemon twist.

Ibiza Sunset

This zero-proof summer drink was invented by Vivi C Luck, who's been working on her mixology skills since she was knee-high to a bar spoon. Her dad's tequila-based cocktail is on page 33, but this alcohol-free mocktail is perfect for anyone looking for a hot-weather refresher that's fun to make and drink. It's made with just two ingredients: there's a scarlet pool of grenadine syrup that floats at the bottom of the glass, and above it, sparkling lemonade. An orange wheel hangs in the glass like the sun setting over San Antonio Bay. It's very easy to prepare, so if you have any budding mixologists who'd like to try making a simple but stylish non-alcoholic drink, this mocktail is the perfect place to start.

15ml (½fl oz) grenadine syrup
150ml (5¼fl oz) sparkling lemonade, chilled
Orange wheel, to garnish

INSTRUCTIONS

Half-fill a collins glass with ice. Pour in the grenadine syrup, then top up with the chilled lemonade – the grenadine is heavier than the lemonade, so it will sink to the bottom. Tuck the orange wheel into the glass, so it floats just above the crimson layer of grenadine. Serve with reusable straws, so you can stir the grenadine into the lemonade just before you drink it.

Passion Flower

Fans of Porn Star Martinis will love this refreshingly fruity mixed drink. It's made with all the same ingredients as the world-famous martini, but instead of shaking them into a short drink that's served up with a shot of fizz on the side, they're mixed together to make a longer, more thirst-quenching cocktail with a delicate sparkle, thanks to the prosecco top. I don't always think garnishes are essential when mixing cocktails at home, but dropping a lime wheel into the glass just before serving is crucial here. When you bring the glass to your mouth you'll breathe in the vibrant scent of the lime as you take your first sip. The sharp lime and the tangy passion fruit pair beautifully, and enhance the crisp and zingy notes in the cocktail.

1 ripe passion fruit
50ml (1¾fl oz) vanilla vodka
15ml (½fl oz) passion fruit liqueur
15ml (½fl oz) fresh lime juice
50ml (1¾fl oz) dry prosecco, chilled
Lime wheel, to garnish

INSTRUCTIONS

Halve the passion fruit and scoop the pulp into a cocktail shaker. Pour in the vanilla vodka, passion fruit liqueur and lime juice. Add a generous cupful of ice, seal the shaker and shake vigorously for 30 seconds or so until chilled. Fill an old fashioned glass with ice and fine-strain the mix into the glass. Top up with prosecco, lightly stir to mix, then garnish with a lime wheel.

Cherry Baby

This stylish short drink makes the most of one of my favourite flavour combinations: cherries and almonds. The cherry taste comes from the maraschino, a lush liqueur made from Croatian sour cherries that bursts with ripe red flavours. There are two hits of almond in this cocktail: the first comes from amaretto, everyone's favourite almond liqueur from Italy; the second is provided by Crème de Noyaux, a French liqueur that tastes like almonds although it's made from apricot kernels and cherry pits, or stones. It was a popular digestif in the 19th century and it has a creamy marzipan flavour that's backed up with a pinch of peppery spice. The deep red colour comes from cochineal, which gives this cocktail its pretty pink blush. If you can't find Crème de Noyaux in your local bottle shop, simply double up on the amaretto.

45ml (1½fl oz) bourbon
15ml (½fl oz) amaretto
8ml (¼fl oz) Crème de Noyaux
8ml (¼fl oz) maraschino liqueur
2 dashes of chocolate bitters
Maraschino cherry, to garnish

INSTRUCTIONS

Half-fill a mixing glass with ice. Pour in the bourbon, amaretto, Crème de Noyaux and maraschino liqueur. Stir for 1–2 minutes until well chilled. Fill an old fashioned glass with ice. Strain in the Cherry Baby mix. Dash over the chocolate bitters and drop in a maraschino cherry to garnish.

Blueberry & Mint Mojito

Mojitos are one of the easiest summer cocktails you can make at home. The Mojito is built in the glass, layer by layer, so you don't need a cocktail shaker, mixing glass, strainer or even a bar spoon. A wooden spoon will do the work of a muddler to crush the lime wedges, mint and blueberries together, while a regular tablespoon is just as good for stirring the drink as any piece of specialist kit. It's a great drink for cocktail newbies, who'd like to mix up something interesting without investing in barware or risk covering their kitchen in a half-mixed cocktail when the lid flies off the shaker (it happens to us all). A classic Mojito combines mint, lime and sugar with light rum and a dash of soda. This version includes juicy blueberries, which give the drink a pale-purple tinge and pair nicely with the mint. I've upped the amount of soda water added here to create a tall drink that you can sip slowly on warm, sunny days.

12 fresh mint leaves
25g (1oz) blueberries
3 lime wedges
10ml (¼fl oz) Simple Syrup (see page 13)
60ml (2fl oz) light rum
15ml (½fl oz) fresh lime juice
120ml (4fl oz) soda water, chilled

INSTRUCTIONS

Rub the rim of a collins glass with the mint leaves to lightly coat it with the herb's aromatic oils, then drop the leaves into the glass. Add the blueberries and 2 of the lime wedges. Use a muddler or the end of a wooden spoon to crush and muddle them in the glass. Pour in the Simple Syrup and add a large cupful of ice. Stir to mix and chill. Add more ice to the glass and pour in the rum and lime juice. Stir to mix again. Top up with chilled soda water, stir briefly, then garnish with the remaining lime wedge.

Kahlúa & Coke Float

When I started gathering ideas for this book, one of my friends – Gill Penlington – told me about the boozy ice cream floats she had tried at 45 Jermyn St. It's a swish restaurant in London's Mayfair and its cocktail menu has a section devoted to alcoholic ice cream floats. Their chic concoctions combine artisanal ice creams and sorbets with homemade syrups, sodas, spirits and sparkling wines, turning a drink I associate most with children into something refined and elegant. I immediately wanted to create my own tipsy ice cream float, and I wanted it to be aromatic and interesting but also practical – something fragrant and flavourful that I could whip up quickly on a hot day. The solution was to base the drink around cola. We often just think about colas in terms of sweetness, but all colas use a mix of citrus oils and spices to create interestingly fragrant soft drinks. Combining cola with the rich bitterness of Kahlúa and adding some zing from fresh lime juice makes an aromatic soda that is delicious served with creamy vanilla ice cream.

2 scoops of vanilla ice cream
35ml (1¼fl oz) Kahlúa
15ml (½fl oz) fresh lime juice
120ml (4fl oz) cola, chilled

INSTRUCTIONS

Add 2 scoops of vanilla ice cream to a collins glass. Pour over the Kahlúa and lime juice, then top up with the chilled cola. The drink will foam up as you pour, so try to tilt the glass so you're pouring the cola down the side of the glass, rather than directly onto the ice cream. Another way to slow down the foam is to add half the cola, let the foam die down a little, then top up with the remaining cola. Serve the float with reusable straws so you can stir the Kahlúa, cola and ice cream together.

Rosemary Old Fashioned

The Old Fashioned – or the Old Fashioned Whiskey Cocktail, to give it its full name – is said to be the original American cocktail. It dates back to the 1700s, when it was just known as a Whiskey Cocktail. As the centuries passed and other whiskey cocktails went in and out of fashion, this simple mix of whiskey stirred with sugar, bitters and plenty of ice started being referred to as old-fashioned. Somehow that sobriquet stuck and ended up becoming the cocktail's name. But what's fashion when you have style? This herbal take on the Old Fashioned starts the drink with a sprig of fresh rosemary that's bashed until its green, woody fragrance is released. The herb's astringency blends deliciously with the bourbon's mellow oak and vanilla notes. A touch of Honey Syrup and a dash of Angostura bitters complete the cocktail.

2 sprigs of rosemary
60ml (2fl oz) bourbon
8ml (¼fl oz) Honey Syrup (see page 13)
3 dashes of Angostura bitters
Orange wheel, to garnish

INSTRUCTIONS

Place 1 of the rosemary sprigs in a mixing glass and use a muddler or the end of a wooden spoon to bash and crush it until the fragrance is released. Add a generous cupful of ice to the mixing glass. Pour in the bourbon and Honey Syrup and dash in the Angostura bitters. Stir for 1–2 minutes until very well chilled. Add a large ice cube to an old fashioned glass, or simply fill it with ice, and strain in the cocktail. Thread a short rosemary sprig through an orange wheel and place it in the glass to garnish.

Kirsch Royale

For a celebration, nothing beats a champagne cocktail – or prosecco, or cava, or whatever your favourite form of fizz is. This sparkling mixed drink takes the format of the French favourite, Kir Royale, and swaps the crème de cassis for kirsch, a sour cherry schnapps that's popular in German-speaking countries across Europe. Kirsch is fiery but not that sweet, so I've added in a measure of plain Simple Syrup and the syrup from a jar of maraschino cherries to take the heat out of the drink. Combined with sparkling wine, it makes an easy drinking cocktail that's a festive shade of red. What makes this cocktail especially good for celebrations is that you can prepare part of it the day before the event, saving you time and stress when your guests arrive. The syrupy kirsch mixture has to be chilled. It makes up almost one-third of the finished drink, so if it's warm, your cocktail will be warm too – no matter how well-chilled the sparkling wine is. Warm fizz makes for flat parties, so plan ahead.

Serves 6

90ml (3fl oz) kirsch
100ml (3½fl oz) Simple Syrup (see page 13)
90ml (3fl oz) syrup from a jar of maraschino cherries
550ml (18½fl oz) dry sparkling wine, chilled
Maraschino cherries, to garnish

INSTRUCTIONS

Pour the kirsch, Simple Syrup and cherry syrup into a tub or jar, stir to mix, then seal and chill in the fridge for 24 hours. Alternatively, half-fill a mixing glass with ice then pour in the kirsch, Simple Syrup and cherry syrup. Stir well to chill, then strain into a pitcher. To build the cocktails, drop a maraschino cherry into each of 6 flute glasses. Pour approximately 45ml (1½fl oz) of the kirsch mix into each glass. Top up with the chilled sparkling wine.

Rhubarb & Red Vermouth Spritz

Summer is spritz season. In Venice they'll tell you that spritzes are only for drinking before lunch, but I've never found a time of day that doesn't suit a spritz (apart from, maybe, breakfast). The secret is finding the right spritz for the moment. The standard Spritz Veneziano (see page 37) is a great pre-lunch or dinner drink because the bitter flavour perks up your taste buds and starts your tummy rumbling, ready for your meal. But for an afternoon spritz, I prefer a drink with softer flavours and a milder buzz. Sweet red vermouth shares some of the same herbal notes as the more astringent Italian amaros, but they're moderated by hints of vanilla, aromatic spices and sugar. To make it even smoother, I've added rhubarb syrup, as its tart fruitiness is a tasty match with the vermouth.

60ml (2fl oz) sweet vermouth
45ml (1½fl oz) rhubarb syrup
90ml (3fl oz) dry prosecco, chilled
30ml (1fl oz) soda water, to top up
Orange wheel, to garnish

INSTRUCTIONS

Fill a copa, coupe or wine glass with ice. Add the vermouth and rhubarb syrup and stir to mix. Top up with the chilled prosecco and gently stir to mix again. Add the soda water to the glass to top up the drink, then tuck in an orange wheel to garnish.

Bourbon & Peach Smash

Finding drinks that go with a barbecue can be a challenge. There's the richness of the meat, the sugar and spice found in the marinade, the vinegary tang of pickles, the heat from hot sauce – and that's before we even start to think about the smoke. Beer is always a safe bet, but if you want something a little more sophisticated, reach for the bourbon. Characteristically, bourbons feature notes of vanilla, caramel, butterscotch, maple, honey and chocolate. Rich, creamy flavours that lean towards sweet but are backed up by the alcohol's heat. If you're hosting a barbecue, a bottle of bourbon and plenty of ice is a solid drink choice. But if you'd like to make your bourbon go further, turn it into a smash. A bracing mix of mint, sugar and spirits, smashes are invigorating cocktails that are best served over plenty of ice. This Bourbon Smash features fresh peach and peach liqueur, giving it a luscious summery flavour. Don't skip the mint – it gives the drink its bite.

4 fresh mint leaves
2 tbsp fresh peach purée (see page 15)
60ml (2fl oz) bourbon
30ml (1fl oz) fresh lemon juice
15ml (½fl oz) crème de pêche
15ml (½fl oz) Honey Syrup (see page 13)
Peach wedge and mint sprig, to garnish

INSTRUCTIONS

Add the mint leaves to a cocktail shaker and bash them with a muddler or the end of a wooden spoon to bruise and muddle them, releasing their fragrance. Add the remaining ingredients to the shaker with a generous cupful of ice. Seal and shake well for 30 seconds or so until well chilled. Fill an old fashioned glass with ice and fine-strain in the cocktail mix. Garnish with a peach wedge and a sprig of mint.

Strawberries & Cream Martini

This creamy cocktail is what you get when a milkshake dreams of being a Martini. It was inspired by the quintessential summer combination of strawberries and cream – a pairing that's ubiquitous in Britain in the sunny months. Most famously, bowls of strawberries and cream are served to spectators at the annual Wimbledon tennis tournament. The sweet snack has become such an essential part of the Wimbledon experience that the Lawn Tennis Club has kept the price the same since 2010, ensuring that everyone who attends can afford to treat themselves if they want to. Whether you're watching the tennis or just want something indulgent to drink, this cocktail is brimming with berry flavours that fans of summer fruit will adore.

45ml (1½fl oz) vanilla vodka
30ml (1fl oz) single cream
15ml (½fl oz) crème de fraise
8ml (¼fl oz) Simple Syrup (see page 13)
2 tbsp strawberry purée
Strawberry, to garnish

INSTRUCTIONS

Place a martini glass in the freezer for 5–10 minutes to chill, or fill it with ice and set aside to chill. Add a generous cupful of ice to a cocktail shaker and pour in the vanilla vodka, single cream, crème de fraise and Simple Syrup. Add the strawberry purée, seal the shaker and shake well for at least 30 seconds or until well chilled. Discard the ice from the martini glass, if necessary, then fine-strain in the cocktail. Garnish with a strawberry.

Blushing Lady

Many years ago, my friend Francesca Burnett-Hall ordered a Nectarine White Lady in an East London bar and it tasted so much like a nectarine that every sip was almost like taking a bite out of an actual fruit. I've been trying to recreate that experience ever since, combining different mixes of stone fruits, citrus juices and liqueurs. I've never quite managed it, but this fresh and flavoursome cocktail comes close. It's based on a White Lady, but I've added in crème de pêche, then backed that up with Crème de Noyaux, a French liqueur that's made from apricot kernels and cherry pits, or stones. Together they recreate the flavour of a whole peach – both the sweet, juicy flesh and the almond-scented stone. Dotting the top of the cocktail with peach bitters just before serving helps round out that peachy flavour.

45ml (1½fl oz) London dry gin
25ml (¾fl oz) crème de pêche
25ml (¾fl oz) fresh lemon juice
15ml (½fl oz) fresh egg white
8ml (¼fl oz) Crème de Noyaux
Peach bitters, to garnish

INSTRUCTIONS

Place a coupe glass in the freezer for 5–10 minutes to chill, or fill it with ice and set aside to chill. Pour all the ingredients apart from the bitters into a cocktail shaker and add a generous cupful of ice. Seal and shake well for around 30 seconds or until well chilled. Strain into a glass and discard the ice from the shaker. Pour the chilled cocktail mix back into the shaker and shake well for another 30 seconds or until it feels and sounds light. Discard the ice from the coupe glass, if necessary. Strain in the cocktail and dot a row of peach bitter dashes across the top of the drink to garnish.

Flirtini

Without the champagne this cocktail is a French Martini, but add a splash of fizz and suddenly we're getting a little saucy. No surprise then that Flirtinis made an appearance in an episode of *Sex and the City*, where they were served as a pitcher drink during a rooftop barbecue hosted by Samantha. This version is a little bit stronger, hence the single serve. The combination of vodka, crème de framboise and pineapple juice is luscious, but it still has a wicked kick – this cocktail isn't nearly as girlish as the name suggests. After shaking, the drink will separate in the glass into a plummy pink layer topped with a velvety white foam. Pour in a splash of chilled champagne and raise a glass to the good times that are sure to follow.

25ml (¾fl oz) vodka
25ml (¾fl oz) crème de framboise
60ml (2fl oz) pineapple juice
50ml (1¾fl oz) dry champagne, chilled
Fresh raspberries, to garnish

INSTRUCTIONS

Place a martini glass in the freezer for 5–10 minutes to chill, or fill it with ice and set aside to chill. Half-fill a cocktail shaker with ice. Pour in the vodka, crème de framboise and pineapple juice. Seal and shake well until chilled. Discard the ice from the martini glass, if necessary. Strain in the cocktail mix, then top up with the chilled champagne. Thread a couple of raspberries onto a cocktail pick and balance them on the glass to garnish.

Campari G&T

A cross between a Negroni, an Americano and a standard gin and tonic, this generously portioned G&T is ideal as a sundowner, especially as the splash of Campari in the cocktail mimics the colours of a summer sunset. Campari is a bitter liqueur that was invented in Milan in the 1860s. It's flavoured with 68 different herbs and spices that give it a unique astringency that many people find challenging to start with it. But if you persevere, you'll find yourself developing a taste for this herbaceous drink and start seeking out cocktails made with it. Luckily for Campari fans, there are plenty to choose from. In this G&T the Campari adds a nip of bitterness that you can either heighten by pairing it with a London dry gin or smooth out by picking a mellower boutique gin. Whichever you choose, make sure you pack your glass with ice. For long drinks like this G&T, the secret to keeping them cool without diluting them is adding as much ice as possible to the glass. Seems counterintuitive, but in fact the more ice in the glass, the cooler it stays, which means the ice will melt more slowly.

60ml (2fl oz) gin
25ml (¾fl oz) Campari
150ml (5¼fl oz) tonic water, chilled
Orange wheel and rosemary sprig, to garnish

INSTRUCTIONS

Fill a copa glass with ice. Pour in the gin and Campari and stir to mix. Top up the ice, if necessary, then pour in the chilled tonic water. Gently stir to mix. Thread a short rosemary sprig through an orange wheel and place it in the glass to garnish.

Pineapple & Thyme Rum Fizz

Fizz means fun, even when the fizz is coming from a dash of soda water. As a category of cocktail, fizzes are usually made with a spirit, a fruit juice, some sugar and a carbonated soft drink to create long drinks that are ideal for serving on swelteringly hot days. They're the perfect choice when you need a drink that will revitalize you, while also chilling you out. Rum and pineapple juice are famously good together in drinks; in this fizz, their flavours flourish when blended with the woody notes of fresh thyme and a zingy squeeze of lime juice. If you don't like rum, you could swap it for vodka or silver tequila and still get a refreshingly good drink.

1 large sprig of fresh thyme
60ml (2fl oz) light rum
35ml (1¼fl oz) pineapple juice
15ml (½fl oz) fresh lime juice
8ml (¼fl oz) Simple Syrup (see page 13)
Dash of chilled soda water, to top up
Maraschino cherry, to garnish

INSTRUCTIONS
Place the thyme sprig in a cocktail shaker and use a muddler or the end of a wooden spoon to crush it until the fragrance is released. Pour in the rum, pineapple juice, lime juice and Simple Syrup. Add a generous cupful of ice, seal and shake vigorously for around 30 seconds or until well chilled. Fill a highball glass with crushed ice and fine-strain in the cocktail. Top up the glass with a dash of chilled soda water. Drop in a maraschino cherry to garnish.

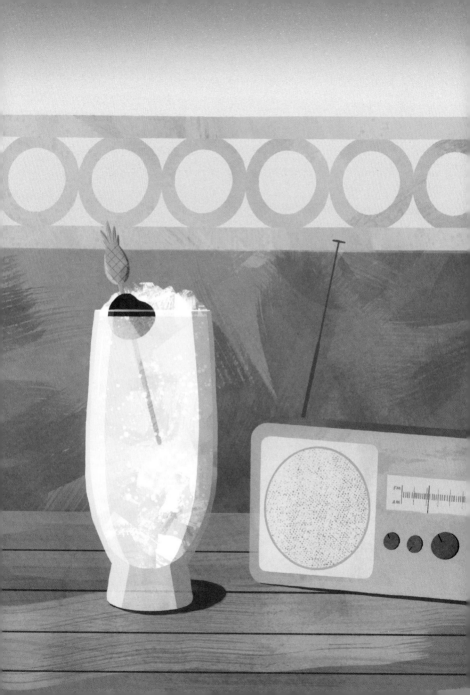

Passion Fruit Daiquiri

Another riff on the Porn Star Martini, but this time I've turned it into a zesty fresh fruit daiquiri. Hailing from Cuba, daiquiris are rum cocktails that – at their most elemental – shake light rum with lime juice and sugar to make a crisply refreshing mixed drink. Daiquiris have been helping to take the heat out of the day in the Caribbean since 1898, so they're a natural choice of drink for summer. This simple recipe is an ideal starting point for mixologists who want to add a few personal flourishes to the original drink. Around the world you'll find daiquiris served frozen, on the rocks, full of fresh fruit, with switched-up spirits, or even just mixed to be twice the standard size (the Papa Doble or Hemingway Special). My Passion Fruit Daiquiri is a bit of a party drink, with a cheeky twist of lime enhancing the tropical fruit flavours, and a bright, zesty finish. If you'd like to turn it into a drink for a party, increase the quantities to match your number of guests, then whizz it in a blender with a scant cup of ice. Serve in rocks glasses over more ice.

1 passion fruit
45ml (1½fl oz) light rum
25ml (¾fl oz) passion fruit liqueur
15ml (½fl oz) fresh lime juice
8ml (¼fl oz) Simple Syrup (see page 13)

INSTRUCTIONS

Place a coupe glass in the freezer for 5–10 minutes to chill, or fill it with ice and set aside to chill. Halve the passion fruit and scoop the pulp from one half into a cocktail shaker. Pour in the remaining ingredients and add a generous cupful of ice. Seal and shake vigorously for around 30 seconds or until well chilled. Discard the ice from the glass, if necessary, then fine-strain the daiquiri into the glass. Float the remaining passion fruit half in the glass to garnish.

Pimm's Cup

Pimm's is what summer tastes like in England. It's the drink you'll be served on arrival at summer weddings, barbecues and parties, and if you go to a music festival or to society events, like the Chelsea Flower Show, Henley Royal Regatta or Wimbledon, there will be a Pimm's bar. The subtly bitter liqueur is gin-based and the traditional pitcher drink is made by mixing Pimm's No 1 Cup with lemonade. This version is made with a mix of lemonade and ginger beer, to add a little fire. I've also added in sweet vermouth and triple sec to pep up the fruit punch. They are optional, and the Pimm's Cup will still be refreshingly delicious without them, but they do add an extra level of flavour. One thing that's not optional is the fruit. If you don't get a mouthful of orange, lemon, mint and berries whenever you take a sip from your glass, then you're not really drinking a Pimm's.

Serves 6

300ml (10fl oz) Pimm's No 1 Cup
150ml (5¼fl oz) sweet vermouth
150ml (5¼fl oz) triple sec
A handful of raspberries
1 orange, thinly sliced
1 lemon, thinly sliced

¼ cucumber, thinly sliced
300ml (10fl oz) sparkling lemonade, chilled
300ml (10fl oz) ginger beer, chilled
A handful of mint sprigs

INSTRUCTIONS

Pour the Pimm's, vermouth and triple sec into a large jug. Add the raspberries and the sliced orange, lemon and cucumber. Set aside for 1 hour to steep – this isn't essential, but steeping the fruit in the Pimm's adds a fresh, fruity flavour to the final drink. When you're ready to serve, half-fill the pitcher with ice and stir to mix with the Pimm's and fruit. Pour in the lemonade and ginger beer. Gently stir to mix again, and tuck in a few sprigs of mint. Serve in ice-filled highball glasses.

Espresso & Tonic

One of the first drinks to be made famous on Instagram, Espresso & Tonic was invented in Sweden in 2007, where it was called Kaffe & Tonic. It was invented by a barista at Koppi, a coffee roasters and café in Helsingborg. It quickly became their best-selling iced coffee and versions of the drink began popping up in cafés and bars across the country. Eventually, the Kaffe & Tonic made its way around the world, thanks to Swedish coffee enthusiasts who shared snaps of the elegant drink on social media. A well-made Espresso & Tonic has a dark layer of espresso floating on top of a clear bubbly pool of tonic. To create the two-tone effect, pour the espresso carefully into the tonic water over the back of a bar spoon. It should slowly drift down through the tonic water, giving you time to take your Insta-friendly shot before stirring the sour espresso into the crisp and invigorating tonic water and taking your first sip.

35ml (1¼fl oz) espresso, cooled
180ml (6fl oz) tonic water, chilled
Maraschino cherry, to garnish

INSTRUCTIONS

Make your espresso (or run to the coffee shop and get them to make one for you), then let it cool. Fill a collins glass with ice and pour in the tonic water. Gently and slowly pour the espresso into the glass over the back of a bar spoon so it swirls through the clear tonic water, then drop in a maraschino cherry to garnish.

Porch Punch

Is there anything bourbon doesn't go with? Over the years I've become more and more fond of this giant among American spirits. Made with corn mash and aged in charred oak barrels, bourbon's flavours range from sweet caramel through hot pepper, cinnamon, honeysuckle and rose petal to almonds and vanilla. This cooling punch benefits from being made with a bourbon that leans towards the floral end of the flavour spectrum, like Four Roses, or a sweeter bourbon, such as Maker's Mark. You'll be mixing it with a breakfast tea blend, which is typically full of robust, punchy flavours. A delicate bourbon will complement the tea, rather than compete with it. Get the combination right and you'll end up with a pitcher drink that's sweet, smoky and invigorating.

Serves 6

4 tbsp English breakfast tea leaves or 4 tea bags
350ml (12fl oz) bourbon
250ml (8½fl oz) fresh peach purée
180ml (6fl oz) Honey Syrup (see page 13)
90ml (3fl oz) fresh lemon juice
Lemon wheels and mint sprigs, to garnish

Instructions

Add the tea to a heatproof jug and pour in 500ml (17fl oz) freshly boiled water. Let the tea steep for 5 minutes, then strain into a clean jug. Top it up with more water if it's now less than 500ml (17fl oz). Set aside to cool. When you're ready to mix the cocktail, half-fill a pitcher with ice. Pour in the bourbon and add the peach purée, Honey Syrup and lemon juice. Stir well for 1–2 minutes to chill and mix. Top up with the tea and stir again. Add a cupful more ice to the pitcher and tuck in some lemon wheels and mint sprigs. Serve over ice in rocks glasses.

Bahama Mama

The Bahama Mama is one of those cocktails that shows up on bar menus around the world without anyone ever knowing exactly where it came from. The first Bahama Mama might have been mixed in a seedy Prohibition bar by a bartender looking for a way to smooth out the rough edges of their bootlegged rum, and they hit on fruit juice and sweet liqueurs as the solution. Or it could have been invented in a Californian tiki bar in the 1930s, shaken together by a Hawaiian-shirted barman selling South Pacific dreams and strong drinks in the sunshine. Maybe it really did come from The Bahamas, where they know their rum and they grow the sweetest pineapples in the world. Wherever and whenever the Bahama Mama was first mixed, there's one thing we can all agree on: nothing tastes more like liquid sunshine than the first sip of this fruity rum punch.

15ml (½fl oz) dark rum
8ml (¼fl oz) 151 proof rum
15ml (½fl oz) coconut rum liqueur
15ml (½fl oz) fresh lemon juice
8ml (¼fl oz) coffee liqueur
90ml (3fl oz) pineapple juice
8ml (¼fl oz) grenadine syrup
Pineapple wedge and maraschino cherry, to garnish

INSTRUCTIONS
Half-fill a cocktail shaker with ice and pour in all the ingredients. Seal and shake well for 30 seconds or until well chilled. Fill a hurricane glass with ice, then strain in the cocktail. Thread a pineapple wedge and a maraschino cherry onto a cocktail pick and balance them on the glass to garnish.

Bloody Maria

Go one better than a Bloody Mary this summer and mix yourself
a Bloody Maria. Made with tequila, the Bloody Maria is less harsh
and more drinkable than the original, vodka-based version. I've used
reposado tequila in this version of the brunch classic. Reposado
tequilas are aged for between two months and one year in barrels,
giving the spirit time to rest (*reposado* means 'rested' in Spanish) and
absorb the flavour of the oak. They typically have a golden colour
and hints of vanilla, sweet spice or woodsmoke. Reposado tequila
is a great choice for cocktails and can be used as an alternative for
silver tequila in any recipe in this book. In this Bloody Maria, the
tequila's creaminess helps to balance out the tomato juice's acidity.
The Jalapeño Simple Syrup has the same function, while also adding
a little spice along with its sweetness. I've used Tabasco to add that
essential touch of fire, but you can swap in your preferred hot sauce.

60ml (2fl oz) reposado tequila
120ml (4fl oz) tomato juice
15ml (½fl oz) fresh lemon juice
15ml (½fl oz) Jalapeño Simple
   Syrup (see page 14)
4 dashes of Worcestershire sauce

4–8 dashes of Tabasco sauce
A pinch of celery salt
A pinch of freshly ground
   black pepper
Celery stick and lemon
   wedge, to garnish

INSTRUCTIONS

Add a cupful of ice to a cocktail shaker. Pour in the tequila, tomato
juice, lemon juice and Jalapeño Simple Syrup. Shake in the
Worcestershire sauce and Tabasco sauce – use as much or as little
Tabasco as you like. Add a pinch each of celery salt and black pepper.
Seal the shaker, then gently slide the cocktail from side to side inside
the shaker, revolving it as you move it backwards and forwards, for
1 minute. Don't shake it, as this will aerate your tomato juice and make
it frothy. Instead, just gently move the cocktail around inside the shaker
to chill it. Fill a collins glass with ice and strain in the Bloody Maria.
Tuck in a celery stick and a lemon wedge to garnish.

Frozen Papaya Daiquiri

I tend to think of frozen cocktails as being a modern invention (or modernish, depending on whether or not you think the 1980s are recent). So, learning that the Frozen Daiquiri was actually invented between 1920 and 1930 was a surprise. The barman who made iced daiquiris famous was Constantino Ribalaigua Vert, who ran the bar at the El Floridita in Havana. Stirring shaved ice back into the drink after it was mixed resulted in a super-chilled cocktail, proving a big hit with the bar's patrons, including Ernest Hemingway, said to have drunk an unbelievable seventeen in one go. The invention of the Waring Blender in 1937 meant the ice could be blended with the cocktail ingredients, and even fruit – with the touch of a button, a new kind of cocktail was created. This Frozen Daiquiri is blended with papaya, which gives the cocktail its neon-orange colour and luxurious velvety texture. Just make sure you peel, chop and freeze your papaya the night before you want to serve the drink, so it's ready to be blitzed into a tropical twist on a classic.

Serves 2

1 papaya, weighing approximately 350g (12oz)
120ml (4fl oz) light rum
50ml (1¾fl oz) fresh lime juice
50ml (1¾fl oz) Simple Syrup (see page 13)
Lime twists, to garnish

INSTRUCTIONS

Halve the papaya, remove the seeds, then scoop the flesh out of the skin into a tub – you should have around 225g (8oz) papaya. Seal and freeze for at least 24 hours. The papaya will keep for up to 3 months in the freezer. To make the daiquiris, scoop 225g (8oz) frozen papaya into a blender and add a cupful of ice. Pour in the rum, lime juice and Simple Syrup. Blitz to make a smooth and creamy mix. Pour into 2 large coupe or margarita glasses. Garnish with lime twists.

Spicy Watermelon & Lime Frosé

Pink, fluffy frosé was 2016's trending drink. It was invented by Justin Sievers in New York's Bar Primi. He blended Sicilian rosé wine, sweet vermouth and strawberries to create a sparkling, slushy cocktail that was half drink and half dessert. A video of Sievers mixing the cocktail went viral and curious drinkers began lining up to try this super-chilled summer drink. Made with a juicy, fruity rosé wine and the right blend of fruit and syrup, the frosé is just as enjoyable as the first time it was mixed on a sticky New York night. This version uses a peppery Jalapeño Simple Syrup, giving the drink a sweet and spicy flavour. If you don't like chilli, use a plain Simple Syrup instead. But don't leave out the syrup or try to reduce it – when things are frozen the flavours are dulled, so this frosé needs the syrup's sweetness and the lime's zinginess to keep the flavours bright.

Serves 8–10

750ml (1.3 pints) fruity rosé wine
400g (14oz) watermelon, chopped
200ml (7fl oz) Jalapeño Simple Syrup (see page 14)
100ml (3½fl oz) fresh lime juice
Lime slices, to garnish

INSTRUCTIONS

Pour the wine into a large, shallow tin or tub and slide into the freezer. Freeze overnight or until slushy – it will take at least 12 hours. When you're ready to mix the frosé, scrape the slushy frozen wine into a blender. Add the chopped watermelon and a generous cupful of ice. Pour in the Jalapeño Simple Syrup and lime juice and blitz until thick and slushy. Pour into rocks glasses and garnish with lime slices. It will melt quickly, so serve straight away.

Caribbean Rum Punch

The classic proportions for rum punch are one of sour (citrus juice), two of sweet (sugar), three of strong (rum) and four of weak (mixers, such as fruit juice, tea, water or soda). It's a handy rhyme to remember when you're mixing drinks. The sweet is split between grenadine and Simple Syrup, so the grenadine's tangy pomegranate flavour doesn't overwhelm the other ingredients. The rum is also split 50:50. There's a mix of light and dark rum, which means you get to enjoy the punchier flavours of the aged dark rum but they're cut by the sweeter light rum, bringing balance to the drink. Stick to this mix of rums or swap for your preferred type. There's another split when it comes to the weak – a combination of fresh orange and pineapple juices. Mixed with all the other ingredients (including the sour lime juice), they make a gluggably good rum punch that's a vibrant burgundy colour and full of spice. Make sure to include the nutmeg, a key part of rum punches for over 400 years, adding a touch of Caribbean warmth.

Serves 6

90ml (3fl oz) fresh lime juice
90ml (3fl oz) grenadine syrup
90ml (3fl oz) Simple Syrup
    (see page 13)
135ml (4½fl oz) light rum
135ml (4½fl oz) dark rum
180ml (6fl oz) pineapple juice

180ml (6fl oz) fresh orange juice
10–12 dashes of Angostura
    bitters
Grated nutmeg, to taste
6 fresh pineapple wedges
    and maraschino cherries,
    to garnish

INSTRUCTIONS

In a pitcher, combine all the ingredients apart from the nutmeg and stir well. Chill in the fridge for 1–2 hours, or overnight. When you're ready to serve, fill 6 hurricane or rocks glasses, with ice. Pour in the rum punch. Grate a little fresh nutmeg over each glass. Thread a pineapple wedge and a maraschino cherry onto 6 cocktail picks and rest them in the glasses to garnish.

Kalimotxo

Also known as Calimocho, the Kalimotxo was invented in
Spain in the 1970s. The story goes that the organizers of a
festival in Algorta, a port town in the Basque region of Spain,
opened up the crates of wine they'd ordered for the event and
realized they'd bought a bad batch of wine. Not willing to let
the wine go to waste – and with no time or money to replace
it – they had to come up with a way of making it palatable.
Thinking quickly, they reached for the Coca-Cola and mixed
the two together, hoping for the best. Luckily, the drink proved
extremely popular with the crowd and it's still a well-liked
drink in Spain today. This doesn't mean you have to dig out a
sour-tasting bottle of wine from your rack in order to mix this
cocktail; a light and fruity red, like a young Garnacha, Gamay
or Lambrusco, is a great pick. The wine's acidity and the cola's
sweetness balance each other out, creating a lower-ABV drink
that's laidback and extremely drinkable.

90ml (3fl oz) red wine
90ml (3fl oz) cola, chilled
Orange twist, to garnish

INSTRUCTIONS
Fill a rocks glass with ice and pour in the red wine and cola.
Briefly stir to mix, then garnish with an orange twist.

Lagerita

If you like Margaritas but are getting a bit bored of the same old flavours, then crack open your beer fridge and try mixing yourself this inspired cocktail, which adds a lager top to a traditional Marg mix. The Lagerita is attributed to Simon Ford, a cocktail expert and brand ambassador who began his cocktail career running Koba, a bar in Brighton on the south coast of the UK that was famous for its quality cocktails. It's a zesty cocktail that's full of effervescent flavour. When picking the lager, go for a light and refreshing variety. If you can get hold of Mexican beers, use Pacifico or Modelo Especial. If not, an easy-drinking lager is a safe bet. Like many of the drinks in this book, I've made it slightly longer than the standard version of this cocktail because I think hot-weather drinks need to be thirst-quenching as well as bracingly boozy. Lively, foam-topped and with a kick of tequila, this beer cocktail is definitely both.

1 tsp fine sea salt
2 lime wedges
50ml (1¾fl oz) silver tequila
25ml (¾fl oz) triple sec
25ml (¾fl oz) fresh lime juice
200ml (7fl oz) Mexican lager, chilled

INSTRUCTIONS

Tip the salt onto a small plate. Rub the rim of a collins glass or beer mug with one of the lime wedges, then press it down into the salt to lightly coat it. This is optional, but even if you don't want the salt rim, rubbing the edge of the glass with the lime wedge ensures that the first sip you take will have a zing of citrus. Pour the tequila, triple sec and lime juice into a cocktail shaker. Half-fill the shaker with ice, seal and shake vigorously until the Margarita mix is well chilled. Half-fill the glass with ice cubes, then strain the mix into the glass. Top up with the chilled lager and drop in the remaining lime wedge to garnish.

White Sangria

When people think of classic summer drinks, Spanish Sangria is always high on the list. A sweetened mix of wine, fruit and liquor, it's the drink that all tourists want to try most when they land in Spain. Typically, Sangria is made with red wine – the name comes from the Spanish word for blood, reflecting the wine's dark ruby colour – but it doesn't have to be. A white Sangria, made with a crisp and acidic white wine, like pinot grigio, sauvignon blanc or a white Garnacha, is just as delicious and refreshing. The three things a good Sangria does need are fruit, an extra wallop of alcohol from a spirit or vermouth, and it has to be cold. This White Sangria is made with a blend of cantaloupe melon juice, which gives the drink a lush richness, Spanish brandy for kick, and ginger ale for sweetness and spice. Try to chill all the ingredients before you mix them together – you are going to add ice, but it helps if everything is cold to start with. This is one of those drinks that is at its best when it is really and truly ice-cold.

Serves 6

300ml (10fl oz) fresh melon (cantaloupe) juice, chilled
120ml (4fl oz) Spanish brandy
750ml (1.3 pints) white wine, chilled
600ml (20fl oz) ginger ale, chilled
Lemon, orange, and lime wheels, to garnish

INSTRUCTIONS

Pour the melon (cantaloupe) juice and brandy into a pitcher and add 2 cupfuls of ice. Stir well to mix, then pour in the white wine and stir again. Top up the pitcher with the ginger ale, then drop in the lemon, lime and orange wheels. Serve the Sangria in ice-filled rocks glasses.

Rosita

A variation on the Negroni, this tart, booze-forward cocktail was developed by gaz regan (sic), a cocktail maestro from Northern England, who made his name mixing drinks in Manhattan. As well as drinks mixer, regan was a prolific writer, and the Rosita appeared in his first book *The Bartender's Bible*, published in 1991. According to some stories, regan forgot about the drink completely, and when a fellow drinks writer served the cocktail at a gathering in the mid-2000s regan asked where the recipe had come from. The host couldn't remember, but later looked it up and reported back to regan that it was from gaz's very own book. The smooth, rounded flavour of the reposado tequila gives this cocktail a richer flavour than the standard Negroni, while the combination of Campari and vermouth brings a mouth-puckering sourness to the drink that keeps it sophisticated.

45ml (1½fl oz) reposado tequila
15ml (½fl oz) Campari
15ml (½fl oz) sweet vermouth
15ml (½fl oz) dry vermouth
A dash of Angostura bitters
Lemon twist, to garnish

INSTRUCTIONS
Fill an old fashioned glass with ice and pour in all the ingredients. Stir well to chill, then top up the ice. Garnish with a lemon twist.

Salted Lime Soda

In India and Pakistan, Nimbu Sodas are ubiquitous. As effective as air conditioning on a hot day, this hydrating citrus drink is an exhilarating mix of sweet, salt and sour. You'll find versions of Nimbu Soda sold across the subcontinent at beach shacks, from market stalls, at restaurants and in fancy hotel bars. It's a drink that crosses boundaries and is welcome at all occasions – when the weather is scorching, who can resist something so refreshing? The simplest version is just a mix of lime juice, salt, sugar and soda water. If you'd like to spice things up, you can add a pinch of chaat masala. But before you do that, try to find black salt – kala namak – and make the drink with that. Kala namak is a rock salt that is mined in the Himalayas then processed by being heated until it melts, is cooled and then aged. It has a unique, sulphurous flavour that gives the Salted Lime Soda its savoury edge. If you add too much you will soon know about it – the eggy pong will overwhelm the drink. So be cautious and start with just ½ teaspoon between four servings. If you like it, up it to 1 teaspoon. More than that and your drink will taste a little too much like a volcano field to be truly delicious.

Serves 4
120ml (4fl oz) fresh lime juice
4 tbsp caster sugar
½–1 tsp black salt
800ml (1.4 pints) soda water, chilled
Lime slices, to garnish

INSTRUCTIONS
Pour the lime juice into a bowl and add the sugar and black salt. Stir well for a few minutes until the sugar has dissolved. Fill 4 highball glasses with ice, then pour in the salted lime juice. Top up each glass with the chilled soda water and gently stir to mix. Garnish with lime slices and serve with reusable straws.

Rhubarb & Lemongrass Fizz

The early 20th century was the Gin Fizz's heyday, when bars would employ battalions of bartenders to shake and serve Gin Fizz after Gin Fizz – it was all their customers wanted to drink. Essentially a long sour, what makes a Gin Fizz different from a Tom Collins (a very similar cocktail) is the serve. Fizzes are always served over crushed ice, and they tend to be a little shorter than the more generously poured Collins cocktails. The drink's simplicity – gin, citrus juice and syrup – means it's easy to adapt and experiment with. This version leans heavily into the citrus, using fresh lemon and lime juice as well as a stick of fragrant lemongrass. Instead of plain Simple Syrup I've used Rhubarb Simple Syrup, as its tart sweetness pairs really well with the gingery warmth of the lemongrass.

Serves 2

1 lemongrass stalk
120ml (4fl oz) London dry gin
30ml (1fl oz) fresh lemon juice
30ml (1fl oz) fresh lime juice
30ml (1fl oz) Rhubarb Simple Syrup (see page 15)
120ml (4fl oz) soda water, chilled
Orange twists, to garnish

INSTRUCTIONS

Trim the woody base off the lemongrass stalk and peel off the tough outer layer. Halve the lemongrass and drop it into a cocktail shaker. Use a muddler, pestle or wooden spoon to bash the lemongrass until the fragrance is released. Pour in the gin, lemon juice, lime juice and Rhubarb Simple Syrup. Add a cupful of ice and seal the shaker. Shake together well. Fill 2 highball glasses with crushed ice and strain in the rhubarb mix, discarding the lemongrass stalk. Top up each glass with a dash of chilled soda water and garnish with an orange twist.

Frozen Hibiscus Margarita

Hibiscus plants grow in tropical and subtropical regions around the world and have been gathered and used to make drinks and medicines for hundreds of years. The petals have a tart flavour that's similar to cranberries and rhubarb, and they're delicious steeped to make a soothing herbal tea. They also make a terrific flavouring for a syrup, imparting a tangy flavour that hits your sweet and sour taste buds simultaneously. For this riff on a Frozen Margarita, you can make your own hibiscus syrup using dried hibiscus flowers (see page 14) or you can use the syrup from a jar of preserved hibiscus flowers. The flavour in the syrup from the jar will be a little more muted, and it won't be the same shockingly pink colour as the homemade syrup, but you'll still get the bright berry notes that pair so well with the fresh lime juice and sweet orange liqueur.

Serves 2

90ml (3fl oz) silver tequila
50ml (1¾fl oz) triple sec
50ml (1¾fl oz) fresh lime juice
30ml (1fl oz) Hibiscus Syrup (bought or
    homemade, see page 14)
6 dashes of orange bitters
Lime slices, to garnish

INSTRUCTIONS

Place 2 margarita glasses in the freezer for 5–10 minutes to chill, or fill with ice and set aside to chill. Pour the tequila, triple sec, lime juice and Hibiscus Syrup into a blender. Dash in the orange bitters and add 2 cups of crushed ice. Blend until smooth. Discard the ice from the margarita glasses, if necessary, and pour in the Frozen Margaritas. Garnish each glass with a lime slice.

Southern Sweet Iced Tea

If you're faced with a warm, humid day that's making you feel sticky and exhausted, then you need to mix up a jug of sweet iced tea. Originally, sweet iced tea was made with green tea leaves. The first recorded recipe for iced tea made with black tea actually comes from Boston. Mary Lincoln, director of the Boston Cooking School, published a recipe for iced tea in her wide-ranging cookbook *Mrs Lincoln's Cook Book: What To Do and What Not To Do in Cooking* in 1884. Lincoln's method involves brewing the tea, letting it cool, then adding it to a glass with sugar and lemon. If you want to let your guests add their own sugar, you can follow this method and serve the iced tea with a bottle of Simple Syrup on the side. But, if you're serving a crowd, it's easier to mix the tea in a pitcher and sweeten it while the tea is hot. The secret to a smooth iced tea is to add a little bicarbonate of soda (baking soda) to the tea while it brews. The soda binds with some of the tannins in the tea, reducing its cloudiness and astringency, helping to create a clear brew with a rounded flavour. There is another secret, and that's not stewing the tea by steeping it for too long. Five minutes is normally enough time to extract the flavour from the tea, while leaving the bitterness behind.

Serves 4

15g (½oz) black tea leaves or 4 tea bags
½ tsp bicarbonate of soda
100g (3½oz) white sugar
Lemon wheels, to garnish

INSTRUCTIONS

Place the tea and bicarbonate of soda in a heatproof pitcher and cover with 1¾ litres (3.2 pints) boiled water. Let it steep for 5–6 minutes, then strain into a clean pitcher and stir in the sugar to dissolve it. Taste and add more sugar, if you think it needs it. Set aside to cool for at least 30 minutes. When you're ready to make the tea, fill a pitcher with ice and pour in the tea. Tuck lemon wheels into the pitcher and serve in highball glasses with extra ice.

Paloma

The most popular cocktail in Mexico isn't the Margarita, it's the Paloma. The name means 'dove' in Spanish, and some people think it got its name from *La Paloma*, a popular 19th-century folk song. Others say that it's a mangling of the Spanish word *pomelo*, which means grapefruit – and which hints that the Paloma was actually invented in America, rather than south of the border. Like many classic cocktails, the drink's actual origins are unclear, but combining tequila with sweet sodas has long been popular in Mexico. In 1955, an American company began exporting a grapefruit-flavoured soda named Squirt to Mexico and that's when the mixture of tequila and grapefruit seems to have really taken off. At its simplest, the Paloma is a combination of grapefruit soda and tequila, but over the years the drink has been tweaked and refined. Fresh grapefruit juice, other fruit juices and sweeteners have all been added into the mix. The result is a deliciously mellow blend of tequila and citrus that will convince the most hardened of tequila haters to change their mind.

60ml (2fl oz) silver tequila
25ml (¾fl oz) fresh grapefruit juice
15ml (½fl oz) fresh lime juice
8ml (¼fl oz) agave syrup
60ml (2fl oz) sparkling grapefruit soda, chilled
Grapefruit wedge, to garnish

INSTRUCTIONS

Half-fill a cocktail shaker with ice. Add the tequila, grapefruit juice, lime juice and agave syrup to the shaker, seal and shake well for around 30 seconds or until well chilled. Fill a collins glass with ice. Strain in the Paloma mix and top up with the chilled grapefruit soda. Briefly stir and garnish with a grapefruit wedge.

Limoncello Spritz

We're reaching a point where it's difficult to imagine a spirit or liqueur that can't be turned into a spritz. If it goes with prosecco (and what doesn't?) then I say we spritz it. This summery spritz is made with limoncello, the zippy lemon liqueur from Italy that is brought out at the end of meals in Italian restaurants as a digestif. Limoncello is said to have been invented on an island off the Amalfi coast in 1900. Maria Antonia Farace grew orange and lemon trees in the garden of a boarding house and turned the citrus skins into a sumptuous lemon liqueur that was served in local restaurants. Her grandson, Massimo Canale, saw the value in his nonna's recipe, trademarked it and began producing the drink on a grander scale. The best limoncello is made with lemons from Amalfi, which are sweeter and juicier than standard lemons and have a thick, knobbly skin that's loaded with the aromatic oils that give lemons their zest. Because limoncello is sweet, I've deviated from the traditional 3:2:1 spritz formula and used a little more soda water than normal. This helps to lengthen out the liqueur's sugariness and stops the drink being too cloying. Experiment with the ratios until you find the version that works best for you.

60ml (2fl oz) limoncello
90ml (3fl oz) dry prosecco, chilled
50ml (1¾fl oz) soda water, chilled
Lemon wheel, to garnish

INSTRUCTIONS
Fill a wine or copa glass with ice. Pour in the limoncello, then top up with the prosecco. Stir briefly to mix. Top up with the chilled soda water. Stir again briefly, then tuck in a lemon wheel to garnish.

Michelada

Sometimes referred to as the Mexican alternative to the Bloody Mary, the Michelada has grown in popularity around the world since the mid-2000s. The first Michelada was a simple affair – a glass of beer served with ice and lime juice in a country club in San Luis Potosí, Central Mexico. It was a hot day and the club member who requested the drink thought it would be refreshing. It must've worked, because more and more people began asking the club barmen for lime in their lager. From the 1970s original, the drink developed to include a salt rim, a dash of hot sauce, sometimes some Maggi sauce and occasionally Worcestershire sauce. Tomato juice, a splash of Clamato and a dash of soy sauce have all been added. As the drink grew in popularity across the border in the USA, it became more elaborate. You'll find bars serving Micheladas loaded with fresh seafood, chunks of tropical fruit and sugary Mexican candies. My version is not quite so elaborate, although I have used Tajin seasoning to rim the glass – a combination of salt, chilli and dried lime that adds lip-tingling spice to the drink.

1 lime wedge
A few pinches of Tajin seasoning
60ml (2fl oz) fresh lime juice
A few dashes of hot sauce
1 tsp Worcestershire sauce
330ml (11½fl oz) Mexican lager, chilled
Lime slice, to garnish

INSTRUCTIONS

Rub the rim of a beer glass or collins glass with a lime wedge, then dip it in the Tajin seasoning to lightly coat it. Pour the lime juice, hot sauce and Worcestershire sauce into the glass and stir together to mix, then top up with the chilled lager. Garnish the glass with a lime slice and serve.

Limonana

Limonana is a Middle Eastern mint lemonade that started off as an advertising stunt in the 1990s. The idea of the drink was created by an Israeli advertising agency that wanted to prove how effective its bus campaigns were. They ran ads on the side of buses for 'limonana', a refreshing iced drink made from lemon (limon) and mint (nana). The ads created a huge buzz and, thrilled by the success of the campaign, the agency revealed it was all a hoax. There was no such drink. Except now, there was. So many people had gone into bars and cafés asking for a Limonana that people had begun creating their own versions of the fictional soda. The drinks ranged from softly sparkling lemonades with a tingly hint of mint to bright green, brain-freezing slushies. This version is syrupy and heavy on the mint – perfect when the sun is shining and the heat is rising.

35ml (1¼fl oz) Mint Simple Syrup (see page 14)
22ml (¾fl oz) fresh lemon juice
½ tsp orange flower water
Chilled sparkling water, to top up
Mint sprigs, to garnish

INSTRUCTIONS
Fill a collins glass with ice cubes. Pour in the Mint Simple Syrup, lemon juice and orange flower water and gently stir to mix. Top up with chilled sparkling water, stir a couple of times, then tuck in a couple of mint sprigs to garnish. Serve with reusable straws.

Lemon, Lime & Bitters

If I asked you to think of a drink that you'd associate with Australia, you might automatically imagine cold tinnies of lager or maybe a flat white. But there is a drink that was invented in Australia and is so ubiquitous that, in Oz, it's known by just its initials – the LLB. Australians drink over 100 million LLBs every year and this pale-orange soft drink is most associated with golf clubs, although it's been around for a lot longer than the oldest Aussie golf green. The drink started off as lemonade and bitters, a non-alcoholic riff on the gin and bitters that British sailors drank to ward off sea sickness and cope with the rigours of life on board ship during the 19th century. In a hot country like Australia, hydration is more important than booze, so the gin was swapped for a tall glass of lemonade pepped up by an herbaceous dash of bitters. In the early 20th century, someone had the genius idea of adding fresh lime juice to lemonade and bitters. No one knows who, although Australian golf clubs are popularly thought to have led the trend. The addition of lime juice adds a pleasing sour note to the drink, sharpening it up and making it more sophisticated than the average glass of lemonade.

20ml (¾fl oz) fresh lime juice
20ml (¾fl oz) fresh lemon juice
250ml (8½fl oz) sparkling lemonade, chilled
4–6 dashes of Angostura bitters
Lime wedge, to garnish

INSTRUCTIONS
Fill a collins glass with ice. Pour in the lime and lemon juices, then pour in the chilled lemonade. Dash in the Angostura bitters and gently stir to mix. Garnish with a lime wedge and serve with reusable straws.

Rose & Cardamom Lassi

Lassis are silky, blended drinks that combine tangy yogurt with water and fruit and sugar, or salt and spices, to make a frothy, foamy refreshment that's as reviving as it is delicious. Originating in the Punjab, there are references to lassis that date back to 1000 BCE, making this one of the oldest mixed drinks in existence. This lassi is sweet, although I have included a small pinch of salt because it enhances the flavours and adds balance to the drink. The combination of homemade Rose Simple Syrup (see page 14) and rose water gives this lassi a romantically floral flavour. When you're shopping for rose water, opt for a flower water that has been made by distilling rose petals rather than created using synthetic flavourings. It will be a little more expensive, but the flavour will be so intense that a little will go a long way. The rose is paired with dusky, freshly ground cardamom, creating a gently perfumed drink.

Serves 2

4 green cardamom pods
400g (14oz) full-fat natural yogurt
2 tbsp Rose Simple Syrup (see page 14)
1 tbsp rose water
1 tbsp caster (superfine) sugar
½ tsp sea salt
Slivered pistachios, to garnish

INSTRUCTIONS

Crack open the cardamom pods in a pestle and mortar. Discard the papery husks and grind the black seeds into a fine powder. Scoop the ground cardamom into a blender. Add the yogurt, Rose Simple Syrup, rose water, caster (superfine) sugar and sea salt with a generous cupful of ice. Whizz together until smooth. Check the lassi – if it seems too thick, add more ice or 2–3 tablespoons of cold water and whizz again. If it isn't sweet enough, add more sugar and blend again. When you're happy with the mix, pour it into 2 highball glasses and sprinkle with slivered pistachios.

Twinkle

The Twinkle was invented by Tony Conigliaro in 2002, when he was working at the Lonsdale Bar in London. Conigliaro's original version of the drink was made with a generous measure of non-alcoholic elderflower cordial. Since then, sweetly perfumed elderflower liqueurs have arrived on the market and the drink has been revised with a smaller, but punchier, measure of liqueur replacing the cordial. When you're mixing this drink, make sure you use a good-quality vodka – the best you can afford. The vodka is the star of the show, so choose a smooth spirit with a mellow flavour that will meld with the floral notes in the elderflower liqueur and the biscuity crispness of the champagne. I think this is a really good brunch cocktail, in spite of its strength. Being served alongside pancakes, eggs and bacon helps soak up some of the booze. The champagne top also adds glamour, so it's a great welcome drink for parties – just make sure there are plenty of canapés to go alongside it.

15ml (½fl oz) elderflower liqueur
25ml (¾fl oz) vodka
45ml (1½fl oz) champagne, chilled
Lemon twist, to garnish

INSTRUCTIONS

Place a small coupe or Nick & Nora glass in the freezer for 5–10 minutes to chill, or fill with ice and set aside to chill. Half-fill a cocktail shaker with ice and pour in the elderflower liqueur and vodka. Seal and shake well for around 30 seconds or until well chilled. Discard the ice from the glass, if necessary. Strain the mix into the glass and top up with the champagne. Garnish with a lemon twist.

White Port & Tonic

Porto Tónico is to Portugal what the spritz is to Italy and the G&T is to Britain. It's a bridging drink that takes you from the end of the working day through to dinner, when long, lower-alcohol mixed drinks like a Port & Tonic are swapped for robust glasses of wine. We tend to think of port as being made with red wines, but white ports are growing in popularity. It's made the same way as its red counterpart, with brandy added to the barrels to stop the fermentation, fortifying the wine and leaving residual sugars behind that make it sweeter than normal table wines. You can get both sweet and dry white ports, and for this cocktail you'll want a dry white port. Look for a young white port that hasn't been aged in the barrel. The port's crisp, herbaceous flavours are similar to vermouth, but without the bitterness, making this cocktail easy to sip. The standard ratio for Porto Tónico is two parts tonic to one part port, but you can play around with the mix. Reduce the amount of port for a longer, lighter drink that has just a touch of alcohol, or go for a 1:1 mix for a stronger drink that lets the flavours of the port really unfurl.

60ml (2fl oz) white port
120ml (4fl oz) tonic water, chilled
Orange wheel, to garnish

INSTRUCTIONS

Fill a collins glass with ice. Pour in the white port, then top up with the tonic water. Stir to mix and garnish with an orange wheel.

Piña Colada

Puerto Rico's national drink, the Piña Colada is a byword for tropical holidays, endless sunshine and long, lazy days on the beach. There are three Puerto Rican barmen who lay claim to mixing the very first Piña Colada. Ramón Marrero Pérez says he was the first person to combine rum, cream of coconut and pineapple juice at the Caribe Hilton Hotel's Beachcomber Bar in the 1950s. Ricardo Garcia agrees that the Caribe Hilton is where the original Piña Colada was mixed, but that he was the one to do it. While Ramón Portas Mingot insists he created the cocktail in 1963 at the Barrachina Restaurant in Old San Juan. Perhaps they all played a part, mixing different quantities of the three key ingredients and eventually giving the drink its name (which means 'strained pineapple'). It would make sense for this crowd-pleasing cocktail to be a group effort. It's the perfect drink for parties – fun, frothy and lightly boozy.

Serves 4

250ml (8½fl oz) light rum
500ml (17fl oz) pineapple juice
200g (7oz) coconut cream
60ml (2fl oz) fresh lime juice
4 fresh pineapple wedges and maraschino cherries,
    to garnish

INSTRUCTIONS

Pour the rum and pineapple juice into a blender. Crumble in the coconut cream (or scoop it in, if it's liquid) and add the lime juice. Add 2 cups of ice and blitz until smooth and slushy. Pour into 4 poco grande, hurricane or collins glasses. Thread pineapple wedges and maraschino cherries onto cocktail picks and rest them in the glasses to garnish.

Tinto de Verano

Similar to Sangria but quicker to make, Tinto de Verano is the wine cooler the Spanish prefer to drink after work during the hot summer months. Its name means 'red wine of the summer' and, unlike Sangria, which typically needs a few hours to macerate the chopped fruit in the wine, Tinto de Verano is mixed and served straightaway. It's easy to drink and best made with a light, fruity red wine like a young Garnacha or pinot noir. Although, if you're feeling bold and would like a little more tannic punch in your Tinto, you can try making it with a cabernet sauvignon or tempranillo. Tintos served in bars and restaurants are normally just a 50:50 mix of red wine and lemonade. I've added a generous measure of sweet red vermouth, to give the flavours an herbaceous boost. Feel free to leave it out (and definitely leave it out if you're using a more tannin-heavy red wine). Just make sure there's plenty of ice and – hopefully – a sliver of sunshine to go with your glass of summer wine.

Serves 6

350ml (12fl oz) fruity red wine
350ml (12fl oz) sparkling lemonade, chilled
180ml (6fl oz) sweet vermouth
Orange and lemon slices or wheels,
    to garnish

INSTRUCTIONS

Half-fill a pitcher with ice, then pour in the red wine, lemonade and sweet vermouth. Gently stir to mix. Add a handful each of orange and lemon slices to the jug and stir to mix again. Serve in tumblers filled with ice. Garnish with orange and lemon slices or wheels.

Index

Acknowledgements

Huge thanks to Gill Penlington and Francesca Burnett-Hall for providing me with inspirations for drinks in this book, and thank you to Jay C Luck and Vivi C Luck for generously sharing their cocktail recipes with me. I'm grateful Naomi and Andrew Knill let me experiment on them yet again, as did my family – my sisters Cara and Alex, my mum Gerry and my dad Doug always volunteer to be drink guinea pigs and I appreciate it. And thank you to my niece and nephew Liam and Niamh, who are much too little to drink but way too cute not to get out a shout-out.

Thank you to my editor Caitlin Doyle, who has tirelessly championed this book and is always a source of wisdom when I get too carried away, and to Sarah Vaughan for her encouragement. Thank you to Sarah Ferone, whose illustrations bring the recipes to life and turn this book into a work of art. Thank you to Jacqui Caulton for her excellent design, as well as the wonderful editorial team of Helena Caldon, Ben Murphy and Rachel Malig.